At the End of an Age

Books by John Lukacs

The Great Powers and Eastern Europe

Tocqueville: The European Revolution
and Correspondence with Gobineau (editor)

A History of the Cold War

Decline and Rise of Europe

A New History of the Cold War

Historical Consciousness

The Passing of the Modern Age

A Sketch of the History of Chestnut Hill College, 1924–1974

The Last European War, 1939–1941

1945: Year Zero

Philadelphia: Patricians and Philistines, 1900–1950

Outgrowing Democracy: A History of the
United States in the Twentieth Century

Budapest 1900: A Historical Portrait of a
City and Its Culture

Confessions of an Original Sinner

The Duel: 10 May–31 July; The Eighty-Day
Struggle Between Churchill and Hitler

The End of the Twentieth Century and the
End of the Modern Age

Destinations Past

George F. Kennan and the Origins of Containment,
1944–1946: The Kennan-Lukacs Correspondence

The Hitler of History

A Thread of Years

Five Days in London, May 1940

A Student's Guide to the Study of History

JOHN LUKACS

At the End
of an Age

Yale University Press • New Haven & London

Designed by Sonia Shannon and set in Galliard type
by Keystone Typesetting, Inc.
Printed in the United States of America
by R.R. Donnelley & Sons.

Library of Congress Cataloging-in-Publication Data
Lukacs, John, 1924–
At the end of an age / John Lukacs.
p.   cm.
Includes bibliographical references and index.
ISBN 0-300-09296-2 (cloth : alk. paper)
ISBN 0-300-10161-9 (pbk. : alk. paper)
1. Civilization, Modern — 1950 — Philosophy.
2. Postmodernism. 3. Science and civilization.
4. Dualism. 5. Monism. I. Title.
CB430 .L85 2002   2001046558
121 — dc21

A catalogue record for this book is available from
the British Library.

The paper in this book meets the guidelines for
permanence and durability of the Committee on
Production Guidelines for Book Longevity of the
Council on Library Resources.

10   9   8   7   6   5   4   3

For my children

Contents

Contents

A Brief Introduction

This book is an essay, without scientific or scholarly presumptions. Its shortcomings include the condition that it is — though only in a few instances — a conclusion of certain convictions expressed in two or three earlier books of mine (*Historical Consciousness,* first published in 1968, twice reprinted since; *The Passing of the Modern Age,* 1970; and *Confessions of an Original Sinner,* 1990, reprinted 2000), of which only the first could be considered a scholarly volume. What compelled me to turn to this present book is set forth, briefly, in the first pages of the first four of its five chapters, wherefore there is no reason for a further Introduction.

However — I tend to muse upon what John Morley wrote 130 years ago: "And a man will be already in no mean paradise, if at the hour of sunset a good hope can fall on him like harmonies of music, that the earth shall still be fair, and the happiness of every feeling creature still receive a constant augmentation, and each good cause yet find worthy defenders, when the memory of his own poor name and personality has long been blotted out of the brief recollection of men for ever." Oh Morley! Talking through his beard! What a Victorian beard that was! Of course there are optimistic and pessimistic beards. (Somewhat later Morley decided to shave off his beard entirely.) And 130 years later can I (beardless) have such a "good hope," at the hour of sunset of a life that occurs together with the going out of the lights of an entire great age and with the swift coming of the incalculable darkness of a new one?

Not like Morley's man.

But: perhaps — which is why I wrote this book.

A Few Acknowledgments

"At the hour of sunset" fewer and fewer friends remain, and they become more and more precious as the years pass. Philip Bell, Bob Ferrell, Don Detwiler, Joanna Shaw Myers: I burdened each of them with the wearisome task of reading a particular chapter of the first drafts of my manuscript. Their comments were invaluable — as was that of yet another old friend, the Norwegian physicist Torger Holtsmark. Then the entire manuscript was read by Jacques Barzun and by my wife, Stephanie, and by my son Paul. Their patient and precise criticisms and reminders were not marginal: they were essential.

I am indebted also to Stephen Breedlove, research librarian of the La Salle University Library, who, marvelously, procured for me books and articles from often far distant and very obscure origins and places; and to Dr. Helen Hayes, who had to struggle (again) with the typing of a clear copy from an exceptionally confusing, scribbled-over manuscript.

1999–2001

ONE
At the End of an Age

✦

"A civilization disappears with the kind of
man, the type of humanity, that has issued
from it."
Georges Bernanos

Convictions: A personal envoi. • The evolution of "modern." • Main features of the Modern Age. • Contradictory dualities. • "Postmodern." • The need to rethink the current idea of "Progress."

For a long time I have been convinced that we in the West are living near the end of an entire age, the age that began about five hundred years ago. This is a prejudice, in the literal sense of that word: a prejudice, rather than a preoccupation[1] — which is why I must sum up, in the briefest possible manner, its evolution.

I knew, at a very early age, that "the West" was better than "the East" — especially better than Russia and Communism. I had read Spengler: but I believed that the Anglo-American victory over the Third Reich (and over Japan) was, at least in *some* ways, a refutation of the categorical German proposition

1. A prejudice is a (not necessarily advantageous) mental illumination; a preoccupation is a mental burden. (Tocqueville somewhere: "To run counter a common opinion because we believe it to be false, is noble and virtuous; but to despise a prejudice merely because it is inconvenient to ourselves, is nearly as dangerous to morality as to abandon a true principle for the same reason.")

3

of the inevitable and imminent Decline of the West. However — Churchill's and Roosevelt's victory had to be shared with
Stalin. The result, after 1945, was my early decision to flee from
a not yet wholly Sovietized Hungary to the United States, at
the age of twenty-two. And twenty-odd years later, at the
age of forty-five, I was convinced that the entire Modern Age
was crumbling fast. The result was a short book entitled *The
Passing of the Modern Age,* published in 1970. During the following thirty years statements about the end of an age appeared
in many of the dozen volumes and other essays and articles
I was writing, on very different topics. Something drove me
to make such statements. I now realize that they almost always appeared in paragraphs at or very near the end of my
various books.

But there is a duality in every human life, in every human
character. I am neither a cynic nor a categorical pessimist. In my
auto-history (it is not really an autobiography) twelve years ago
I wrote — and now see: again on its last page: "Because of the
goodness of God I have had a happy unhappy life, which is
preferable to an unhappy happy one." I wrote too: "So living
during the decline of the West — and being much aware of it — is
not at all that hopeless and terrible." During the ten years that
followed I wrote more books; and since the collapse of Communism (I had seen that coming decades before) I have had the
unexpected experience of seeing book after book of mine translated and published and bought by many readers in my native
country. But during these past ten years (not *fin-de-siècle: fin
d'une ère*) — my conviction hardened further, into an unquestioning belief not only that the entire age, and the civilization to

which I have belonged, were passing but that we are living through — if not already beyond — its very end.

I am writing about the so-called Modern Age, a familiar term which is nonetheless rather inaccurate.[2] For one thing, the Ancient-Medieval-Modern chronological division is not applicable to countries and civilizations beyond the Western world. It was inaccurate when it first arose in the consciousness and in the usage of our ancestors, and it has become ever less accurate since. The word "modern" first appeared in English about four hundred years ago, circa 1580. At first its sense was close to the original Latin *modernus:* "today's," "present." (Shakespeare occasionally used it, meaning "now common.") Gradually the weight of its sense shifted a bit forward, including the meaning of "new" — that is, something different from "old." By the end of the seventeenth century, in English but also in some other Western European languages, another allied meaning became current among learned people, a concept which was one of the results of the emergence of historical consciousness. This was the recognition that there have been three historic ages, the Ancient, the Middle, and now the Modern — whence "medieval," having been in the middle, between the Ancient and the Modern.

There came another shift of consciousness — indeed, of thinking. This was the sense that this modern age might last for

2. In England, "modern history" for a long time meant non-Ancient. In German the Modern Age does not carry that adjective: it is "Neuzeit," literally "New Age." This is also so in a few other languages.

a very long time — indeed, perhaps forever. This was seldom expressed definitely, but there it was: it existed (as it still exists today) in the inability, or perhaps in the unwillingness, of people to contemplate that, like the other ages of mankind, the Modern Age too may or will come to an end. It existed (as it still exists today) in the minds of those who, by and large, equated the Modern Age with an age of increasing Reason — contrasted with the Dark and/or Middle Ages, Ages of Faith. One classic example of this (then not unreasonable) optimism may be found in a passage by Gibbon, who in a stately meandering[3] from his majestic theme, the *Decline and Fall of the Roman Empire,* wrote around 1776: "It may be safely presumed that no people, unless the face of nature is changed, will relapse into their original barbarism. . . . We may therefore acquiesce in the pleasing conclusion that every age of the world has increased, and still increases, the real wealth, the happiness, the knowledge, and perhaps the virtue, of the human race."

Gibbon died five years after the French Revolution, in 1794, the year of Terror. He was not spared the sight of barbarism arising in the midst of Western European civilization, coming from the inside. He did not comment on that, for which we cannot blame him; but at this point we ought to give some thought to the words — that is, to the meanings — of barbarian/barbarism; primitive/primitivism; civilization/culture. The meaning of the first goes back to the Greeks; but the last two are products of the Modern Age. For the Greeks "barbarians" were, by and large, people who were not Greeks — that is,

3. Sheridan on Gibbon: "Luminous? I meant *vo*luminous."

outside and beyond their civilization, a lodgment in space. But *our* usage of "barbarian" or "barbarism" is also — if not mostly — directed to people and behavior and acts in our midst, to people who are "uncivilized" (or, as Russians strangely put it, "uncultured"). Such a meaning is the result not only of experiences but of the emerging historical consciousness at the beginning of the Modern Age, of which an early example is the meaning of "primitive." This word, appearing in English around 1540, first suggested people who are, as yet, "behind" us: that is, behind, rather than beyond, behind us in time, rather than in space: in other words, "retarded." This was another example of the then-changing meaning of Progress (a word that a century or so earlier had meant only advance in space, that is, moving forward). After 1600 the word "civilization" had become the antonym of barbarism and of primitivism ("to civilize: to bring out from rudeness, to educate to civility," *OED* 1601 — again an application of a new meaning of "progress"). Much later, during the second half of the nineteenth and twentieth centuries, a new meaning of "culture" appeared (unlike "civil," the current meaning of "culture" had been unknown to the Greeks and Romans); being "civilized" and "cultured" began to overlap and become sometimes confused. Certain thinkers (mostly Germans, and later especially American intellectuals) would assert that Culture is of a higher order, more important than Civilization — by now, a very questionable assertion.

During the nineteenth century the employment of "modern" was less current; but the optimistic notion of an increasing and possibly everlasting Modern Age was not. What happened was that the notion, and the idea, of Progress had become stronger than the notion, and the idea, of an Age of Reason. Of course, this occurred mainly because of the constantly increasing inventions and productions of applied science. We should recognize that therefore the appearance of the Evolutionary theory of humankind was predictable around 1860. Darwin was not a very original thinker; rather, a man of his time. One of the outcomes of his theory was of course the stretching of the origin of mankind back to hundreds of thousands (and by now, to more than one million) years into a "pre-historic" era. This tendency, perhaps not quite consciously, accorded with a view stretching forward to a perennial, perhaps everlasting, future of mankind; indirectly to a perennial, perhaps everlasting, Modern Age. By the end of the nineteenth century and the beginning of the twentieth, the number of thinkers who, directly or indirectly, began to question this kind of progressive optimism increased. They had their forerunners such as the Neapolitan Vico two centuries earlier; but now there were different writers, such as Nietzsche or Valéry or Spengler, who, in their different ways, tried to remind their readers of the symptoms of decline and of the ultimate fallibility of Western civilization — in the history of which the Modern Age has of course been a part. Finally, during the twentieth century, the appeal of the cult of Reason, of the applications of Progress, and the usage of "modern" itself began to weaken, not only among intellectuals but among more and more people. Toward the end of the century the word "postmodern" appeared, mostly in the abstract realms of literary and art criticism. (To a brief discussion of this belated, confused, and inaccurate designation I must return toward the end of this chapter.)

Meanwhile there exist significant symptoms of an evolving historical consciousness that has no precedents. Because of the achievements of great historians we have acquired a fair amount of knowledge of what had happened — and, perhaps more important, of how people had lived and thought — during the waning of the Ancient and of the Middle Ages. Near the end of the Roman Empire or during the waning of the Middle Ages people knew that some unusual things were happening to them; many of them knew and understood the often worrisome difference of their condition when compared with the lives of their parents or other ancestors; but they seldom thought in terms of the end of an entire age. Yet telling people that we seem to be living near or at the end of an age is no longer something to which they necessarily react with incomprehension or even unexpectedness. Ordinary people, with little knowledge of history, instantly understand when someone, referring to a particular evidence of moral rottenness, says, "It's like the last days of the Roman Empire." This kind of surprisingly widespread (though of course often inaccurate and vague) consciousness of history is a significant symptom. However — every such kind of general historical recognition ought to be sharpened by the understanding of the ending of a very particular age, the one that began about five hundred years ago.

So I must now turn from the evolution (and devolution) of the word "modern" to that of the Modern Age itself. What were its main features?

First of all, it was the *European* Age. There are three sets of reasons for this: geographical, etymological, historical. Until about five hundred years ago the main theater of history was the Mediterranean, and the principal actors were the people along or near its shores, with few important exceptions. With the discovery of the Americas, of the East Indies, of the shape of the globe itself, all this changed. The European age of world history began.

Yet the very adjective, and designation, of "European" was something entirely new at that time, five hundred years ago. The noun "Europe" had existed for a long time, although infrequently used. But "European," designating the inhabitant of a certain continent, was new. (It seems that among the first who invented and used it was Pius II, Aeneas Silvius Piccolomini, a Renaissance Pope around 1470.) In any event: until about five hundred years ago "Christian" and "European" and "white" were almost synonymous, nearly coterminous. There were few inhabitants of the continent who denied that they were Christians. (Exceptions were the Turks in the Balkans, and a small scattering of Jews.) There were very few Christians living outside Europe, and there were few peoples of the white race beyond it, while there were few non-white inhabitants of Europe.

After 1492 "Europe" expanded in several ways. Entire newly discovered continents (the Americas, Australia), as well as the southern tip of Africa, became settled by whites, and Christianized. The lands conquered or colonized by the settlers soon became parts of the empires of their mother countries; the posts and colonies of the European Powers appeared across the world. Finally, European institutions, customs, industries, laws, inventions, buildings spread over most of the world, involving also peoples who were not conquered by Europeans. But after the two world wars of the twentieth century, during which the peoples of Europe grievously wounded each other and themselves, almost all of this came to an end. There were no more new settlements of Europeans (and of whites) on other continents. (One exception is the state of Israel.) To the contrary: the Europeans gave up their colonial empires, and their colonists left their Asian or African homelands. (As late as 1914 the entire continent of Africa, save for two states, Liberia and Abyssinia, belonged to or was governed by a European colonial empire. Eighty years later there was not a single European — or white-ruled — state on the entire continent.) Yet the Christian churches in Africa, Asia, Oceania seem to have survived the reflux of whites, at least in many places. What also survived — indeed, it spread athwart the globe — was the emulation and the adaptation of institutions, industries, customs, forms of art and of expression, laws that were originally European. But the European Age was over.

It was over, at latest by 1945 (if not already by 1917), when the two Superpowers of the world (meeting in the middle of conquered Europe) were the United States and Russia. There remained no European Power comparable to them, not even Britain. This brings up a terminological question. Was (is) the United States European? Yes and no. Yes: in the sense that its origins and laws and institutions — and for about a century the majority of its inhabitants — were of Anglo-Saxon-Celtic origin. No: since its population is now becoming less and less European. And the United States, too, is affected by the crumbling of the institutions and the ideas of the Modern Age that had produced it at its beginning. Indeed, probably more so than many of the states and peoples of Europe. The composition of the American people has been changing rapidly and drastically, whence it is foreseeable that sooner or later whites in America may be a minority. Even more important is the condition that the United States of America was a product of the Modern Age, born in the middle of it—indeed, at its high point—with its ideas and institutions having been largely (though not completely) the results of the eighteenth century Enlightenment.

To list the evidences of the ending of the Modern Age would fill an enormous book. Here I must try to sum up—or, better, to suggest—some of them.

The progressive spreading of democracy has marked the history of mankind, certainly during the past two hundred years but in many ways throughout the entire Modern Age. This progress was usually gradual, at times revolutionary, and not always clearly visible on the surface of world events. How long this democratic age will last no one can tell. What "democracy" really means is another difficult question. But there is a larger consideration. We are living through one of the greatest changes in the entire history of mankind, because until relatively recently history was largely (though never exclusively) "made" by minorities, while increasingly it is "made" by majorities. (In reality it is not so much made by majorities as it is made *in the name* of majorities.) At any rate, this has become the age of popular sovereignty (at least for a while). History has moved from the aristocratic to the democratic era — a passage occurring mostly during the Modern Age, and one that may transcend even the great accepted (Western) scheme of Ancient and Middle and Modern times.

This spread of democracy was the vision of Alexis de Tocqueville; it is present throughout his writings, most clearly in the second volume of *Democracy in America,* where his very method of description was to summarily juxtapose and contrast how society, politics, arts, and even more, mores and manners, formed differently in aristocratic ages before the developing democratic times. And within this very large vision there was a historically more limited one: Tocqueville's recognition, more than a century ago, that this had been and still was a gradual process: with aristocracy declining and democracy rising, the existence of *some* kind of aristocratic order was still necessary to maintain some of the freedoms of otherwise increasingly democratic societies. (That was the main reason for his — of course not unlimited — respect for Victorian England, or even his appreciation of American lawyers whom he once described as an American aristocracy of sorts.) Nearly 175 years later, at the end of the Modern Age, much of this is past. Still the Modern Age *was* marked by the coexistence of aristocracy and democracy, something which has now come to an end.

"Aristocracy" ought not to be categorically defined as the rule of kings and/or noblemen. "Democracy" also means something more than the rule of "the people," more, indeed, than mere popular sovereignty. But especially in Europe, between the highest and the lowest classes (or between the rulers and the ruled) there was another, rather particular, class in the middle: the so-called bourgeois class or classes, whose origins and first influences go back well beyond the beginning of the Modern Age and whose rise marked much of it, together with its achievements. This is not the place to discourse upon either the origins or the meaning of the words "bourgeois" and "bourgeoisie," except that perhaps in most European languages they were linked to the rise and importance of cities. Nor is this the place to expatiate upon the often obscured difference between "bourgeois" and "middle-class." It should be sufficient to observe that by the end of the twentieth century the very term "middle-class" had lost much (if not all) of its meaning because of its tremendous inflationary growth, perhaps especially in the United States but also in other nations where a governing upper class, whether in politics or in society, has practically ceased to exist. Like "modern," "middle-class" is no longer a reasonably accurate category.[4] At the same time, "bourgeois" remains, in retrospect, a historical reality. The existence of a bourgeoisie, especially in Western Europe, and in the English-speaking countries, was not only a sociological phenomenon (or a simple one: since the bourgeois emulated and intermingled with the remaining aristocracies in many ways). It was marked by recognizable forms of behavior and of ideas. We ought to honor its achievements — not only constitutional government and its attempts to balance equality with liberty, but the fact that most of

4 At the other end of the social scale, especially in the United States, the category of a "working-class" as *distinct* from "middle-class" has also largely ceased to exist. What has not ceased to exist is a proletariat of sorts — often a largely non-working one. (As Jesus said: "The poor you will have always with you.") And we now have the New Poor.

the great minds and the greatest artistic creations of the past five hundred years were the products of people of bourgeois origins and of bourgeois status. Which is why it is at least possible and, in my opinion, reasonable to give the Modern Age (or at least its two centuries before 1914) a telling qualifier or adjective: the Bourgeois Age.

The Bourgeois Age was the Age of the State; the Age of Money; the Age of Industry; the Age of the Cities; the Age of Privacy; the Age of the Family; the Age of Schooling; the Age of the Book; the Age of Representation; the Age of Science; and the age of an evolving historical consciousness. Except for the last two, all of these primacies are now fading and declining fast.

The modern state was a product of the Modern Age. Its establishment occurred together with the ideal of civilization: a progress from barbarism. It was a response to, or a result of, the warfare of diverse aristocracies during the fifteenth century, and of the even more injurious religious wars of the sixteenth. The result was the strong, centralized, and sovereign state in most of Western Europe and England, established by absolute or near-absolute monarchs whose rule was especially appreciated by the bourgeois classes, since it provided for their relative safety. Thus royal and centralized absolutism was, especially in its beginnings, an anti-aristocratic, and anti-feudal—to some extent even a democratic—phenomenon. Gradually the democratic element, in this case the bourgeoisie, turned against royal as well as aristocratic power — in England in the seventeenth century, in France in the second half of the eighteenth. Meanwhile — as Tocqueville was the first to point out — the power and the authority of the sovereign and centralized state kept growing, irrespective of whether its sovereignty was represented by a monarch or by a bourgeois government. And due to increasing democracy, in the twentieth century the authority of the state grew further, intending to ensure the material welfare of most of its inhabitants. The existence of "totalitarian" dictatorships in the twentieth century obscured this issue. Their opponents justly feared the limitless and often brutal power of the Total State. Yet Hitler and Mussolini were unopposed by the great majority of their subjects: in sum, they were representatives of popular sovereignty. Hitler himself said that the state was an outdated concept: he was the leader of a people, of a *Volk*, which, in his words, had its primacy over the State. By the second half of the twentieth century, the near-universal principle of government was that of popular sovereignty rather than that of the state; indeed, the power and authority of the state, and respect for it, began to decline. The most evident example of this is Russia, where after the fall of the Soviet Union the problem was no longer the overwhelming power of the state but, to the contrary, its weakness. Elsewhere, too, the break-up of entire states has begun, of which the "privatization" of some of its former functions and services, or the formation of such supra-national institutions as the European Union, are but superficial — and perhaps even transitory — appearances, together with the evident lessening of the authority of the state. Popular resentment against "government" merely masks the essence of

this phenomenon from which the United States is not at all
exempt. An example of this is the increase of criminality, some
of the symptoms of which suggest a new kind of feudalism.
Another more telling example is that while the opponents of
"big government" are the very people who support every ex-
penditure and establishment of "defense" (as if the armed forces
were not part of "government"), successive administrations of
the United States have been both unable and unwilling to protect the very frontiers of the American state, through which
millions of illegal migrants are pouring in.

Money, in one form or another, has always existed; and
money has its history, like everything else; and the Modern Age
has been the age of money — increasingly so, perhaps reaching
its peak around 1900. During the Middle Ages there were some
material assets, often land, that money could not buy; but by
1900 there was hardly any material thing that money could not
buy, while paper money was exchangeable for its equivalent in
silver or gold. But during the twentieth century the value of
money diminished fast. One symptom (and cause) of this was
inflation. When there is more and more of something, its value
becomes less and less; and democracy is probably inseparable
from inflation. Therefore the cyclical rise and fall in the value of
money has largely ceased to exist. That the inflation of words led
to the inflation of money is an important phenomenon, because
the value of every material thing is not only *conditioned* (as a few
economists have at long last become constrained to admit) but
entirely determined by what people think it is; and people think
in words. The inflation of money went apace with the rise of a
general, and historically unprecedented, prosperity; but this

prosperity had little to do with what is still called "capitalism," the latter meaning the preservation and the husbanding of money, rather than the spending of it. By the end of the twentieth century the inflation of stocks and of other financial instruments became even more rapid than the inflation of money — at the bottom of which phenomenon another development exists, which is the increasingly abstract character of money — due, in part, to the increasing reliance on entirely electronic transactions and on their records. Credit cards are but a superficial, though astonishingly widespread, example of this development in a world where income is more important than capital, quick profits more than accumulation of assets, and potentiality more than actuality — that is, creditability more than actual ownership. What has been happening with money is, of course, but part and parcel of a much more profound development: the increasing intrusion of mind into matter. That this happens at a time when philosophies of materialism are still predominant only reflects the mental confusion of our times. In any event, the end of the Modern Age is also the end of the Age of Money — at least as our ancestors used to know it.

The Modern Age was, by and large, marked by an increase in the numbers of people; and by an increase of the production of goods and of their availability. This was of course the result of progress in industry and in agriculture.[5] We now live in a me-

---

5. And of course of trade. Trade was what had led to another characteristic of the Modern Age, to the predominance of sea power. The internal combustion engine changed all of that; during World War II, for example, the decisive importance of land power returned, at least in the European theater of war.

chanical age; but we must recognize that the Age of Industry was remarkably short-lived. It was less than 130 years ago (in 1874) that the majority of people in England were employed in industrial work, not in agricultural production. The people of the United States followed this pattern. But by 1956 the majority of the American population were no longer engaged in any kind of material production, either agricultural or industrial. They were employed in administration and in services. This proportion has grown fast ever since, and in all "advanced" states of the world. (It may be said that the age of democracy has, in reality, devolved into the age of bureaucracy: but not only in "government"; also in every kind of so-called "private" institution.) Of course industry, world-wide, has now been able to produce more and more goods (with varying qualities of durability), employing fewer and fewer people in their mass production. Consider, too, that advertisement and transportation of these goods now cost more (and involve more people) than their production; or that there are entire countries (and some states of the American Union) whose main "industry" is the attraction and management of tourists. It may be said that the production of consumption has become more important than the production of goods.[6] While in the past a respected industrialist was someone who was successful in creating production, now he is someone who creates consumption.[7] What is

6. Evelyn Waugh: "In a democracy men do not seek authority so that they may impose a policy. They seek a policy so that they may impose authority."
7. Perhaps this corresponds to the evolution (or devolution) of republican democracy. The word "democracy" did not appear either in the Declaration of Independence or in the Constitution of the United States. How-

even more telling is that the perception of and the — temporary — use of goods has often become more important than their actual possession.

The Modern Age was the age of the town. The word "bourgeois" is connected to the word for "city" in about every European language (whence the derivation of the word "citizen" — inaccurately, since the latter categorizes the relationship of an individual not to a city but to a state). Bourgeois civilization was largely, though not exclusively, urban. The adjectives "urban" and "urbane" acquired added meanings during the Modern Age. After that the great rise of European and American cities took place. By 1850 London and Paris had more than one million inhabitants each; by 1900 there were more such cities in Europe and three in the United States. This was in part the result of industrialism, whereby millions of men and women left the countryside to find a new life and new work (though often a dreadfully dark and miserable one) in the cities. But there was more than that: the civilization and the culture and the amenities of city life attracted men and women of many kinds. After 1950 the decline of the cities set in. Nearly every great European and American city began to lose population. Within a few decades three dozen or more cities in Asia, Africa, and South America surpassed them in size and in numbers. The once urbane populations had begun to move out of the cities, into the suburbs. These, originally planned to function as

---

ever, by 1828 elections had become popularity contests. This was not what many of the Founders wished to see, but there it was. But then, less than one hundred years later there came a much more lamentable phase: the devolution of *popularity contests* into *publicity contests*.

bridges between city and country living, began to spread and devour both city and countryside. One reason for this was the ubiquity of the personal automobile. Another was the growth of new populations, to whom the civilized proximities and the cultural offerings of cities meant little or nothing. By the end of the twentieth century the association of urbanity with city-living disappeared: the presence of an urbane middle-class within the cities lost its influence and importance.

The Modern Age discovered the virtues — and pleasures — of privacy. Life in the Middle Ages — both in and outside the dwellings of people — was public, in more than one way. Privacy was not an ideal, it was not cherished. Soon after the beginning of the Modern Age there came a change. The most evident material sign of this was the new ideal of the bourgeois house or "apartment" (the latter word is telling: it meant the separation of working and public places apart from private chambers, whether in the palaces of kings or in the houses of the bour-geois). The very word "home" acquired a new meaning. Among other things, the respect for privacy distinguished a civilized society from barbarians or primitive people. This recognition of interiority affected our very language (and our very thinking); the increasing recognition of imagination (arising from the in-side) rather than of "inspiration" (occurring from the outside). Thereafter the increasing emphasis on political and legal rights of the "individual" seemed to affirm the rights to privacy, at least implicitly. But the idea of the private — and thereby autono-mous — "individual" was a fiction. In a mass democratic society (perhaps especially in the United States) the desire for privacy was much weaker than the desire for respectability, usually within a particular community. Compared with the wish for public recognition, the cultivation of private behavior, of private appearances, of private opinions remained confused, occasional, and feeble. The phrase "peer pressure," lately applied to otherwise undisciplined juveniles, has been extant among people well beyond their youth: for the weakness of the ideal of privacy is almost always a sign of insufficient maturity.

The modern cult of privacy had, at first sight, a common ground with the cult of what is still called "individualism" (a questionable term); but at closer sight this connection is deceiving. Privacy had more to do with the developing bourgeois cult of the family. During the Middle Ages children were sent out to work, often for others. During the early Modern Age children returned to the family (or, more accurately, they were kept within the family for a longer time). There were many exceptions to this, especially among certain aristocracies, where children were often extruded from their families, a custom continuing into the eighteenth century. But the tendency to protect and educate children (note the original meaning of "educate": bring up, guide forth) was another new bourgeois habit, eventually spreading up and down, to the nobility as well as to the working classes. Children were no longer treated as little adults or caricatures of adults; there arose, instead, the bourgeois cult of the child — a cult inseparable from the cult of the home, of coziness, of interiority, of privacy.

As the nineteenth century progressed, these bourgeois ideals concerning the protection and the education of children were adopted by various governments. More important: so far as family life went, toward the end of that century for the first time large numbers of married women, including mothers, no longer had to work in the fields or in factories — because of the wages and the industrial employment of their husbands. A working man could afford an apartment or a cottage or even a small house for his family, where his wife would keep house and govern her children; she no longer needed to rise at dawn to go to work elsewhere during the day. Like the entire Industrial Age, this development was short-lived. During the twentieth century came many changes, including the availability of divorce, and of abortion. Yet on many levels, these were consequences rather than causes. As happens before or near the end of a great age, the mutations of institutions, societies, mores, and manners involved the very relations of the sexes. The ideal of the family woman, wife and mother and homemaker, began to fade. Many women, restrained for a long time by certain social customs and habits, became eager to prove their abilities in various kinds of employment: a justifiable aspiration. Yet — especially in the United States — the desire of a woman to be employed somewhere in the so-called "marketplace" was often not the result of financial necessity but, rather, of a new kind of impulse: the life of a housewife — especially in the suburbs — proved to be lonely and boring. Women thought (or, rather, convinced themselves) that they were reacting against the age-old and often senseless categories and assertions of male authority; yet their dissatisfaction often arose not because of the oppressive strength but because of the weakness of males. The rising tide of divorces and abortions, the acceptance of sexual liberties, including pre-marital (and at times post-marital) habits of frequent copulation and other forms of cohabitation, the increasing numbers of unmarried women and single mothers, the dropping birth rate — thus the decline of the so-called "nuclear" family — were, especially after 1955, grave symptoms suggesting vast social changes. They included the perhaps seldom wholly conscious, but more and more evident, tendency of many young women to desire any kind of male companionship, even of a strong and brutal kind, if need be at the cost of their self-respect. In sum, the professional recognition as well as the legal protection of women had risen, while the respect for them had declined. Some of this was due to the twentieth-century cult of youth — which was especially widespread in America during the last phase of its urban and bourgeois period. However, it is not difficult to see that beneath the cult of youth there lurks the fear of death and even the fear of growing up: the fear of having to assume the responsibilities of maturity. The increasing "freedoms" granted to young people in the twentieth century were, in some ways, a return to the practice before the Modern Age, the treatment (or non-treatment) of children as if they were smaller versions of adults. The *education* (in the original sense of that word) of children toward maturity was another bourgeois ideal fading away.

The age of institutional schooling was another feature of the Modern Age. There were universities in the Middle Ages but few (or no) schools of general learning. By the seventeenth century schooling became extended to younger and younger ages, eventually including children of the poor. By the nineteenth century the ideal of general and public education, increasingly involving the responsibility of governments, became sacrosanct. Still, much of the training and the proper education of children remained the responsibility of parents in the home. During the twentieth century this changed. Like so many other things, the role of the schools became inflated and extended, diminishing the earlier responsibilities of parents. In the United States the principal and practical function of the schools often became custodial (especially when both parents were working away from home), though this was seldom acknowledged. After 1960 at least one-fourth of the population of the United States spent more than one-fourth of their entire lifetime in schools, from ages two to twenty-two. As on so many other levels and ways of mass democracy, inflation had set in, diminishing drastically the content and the quality of learning: more and more young people, after twenty years in schools, could not read or write without difficulty. Schools were overcrowded, including colleges and universities. In this increasingly bureaucratized world little more than the possession of various diplomas mattered. Since admission to certain schools — rather than the consequently almost automatic acquisition of degrees — depended on increasingly competitive examinations, the word "meritocracy" was coined, meaning that the rise and positions to be acquired in society depended on the category of the degree and on the category of the college or university wherefrom one graduated: In reality the term "meritocracy" was misleading. As in so many other spheres of life, the rules that governed the practices and functions of schools and universities were bureaucratic rather than meritocratic. It is bureaucracy, not meritocracy, that categorizes the employment of people by their academic degrees. The number and the variation of degrees awarded by higher institutions grew to a fantastic, and nonsensical, extent. Besides being custodial, the purpose of institutional education was now the granting of degrees to provide instant employment.

The inflation of "education" had much to do with the decline of reading (and of its declining requirement in the curricula of the schools). This was another sign of the end of the Modern Age, which was also the Age of the Book. The invention of the printing of books coincided with the beginning of the Modern Age; it was both consequence and cause of many of its achievements. At first it was the availability of books, rather than of schools, that led to an increase of readers — until, by the nineteenth century, men and women who could not read became a small minority among the populations of the Western world. Around the same time the flood of reading matter, including newspapers, rose even higher than the ever-rising flood of books: with the rise of universal literacy (due to the extension of schooling) there was now a new reservoir of potential readers to be tapped. But the inflation of printed matter unavoidably reduced its quality; and there were other influences at hand. The reproduction of more and more pictures in newspapers, magazines, and books; the advent of moving pictures and, finally, of television led to a condition in which — again, not unlike the Middle Ages — the routine imagination of large masses of people became pictorial rather than verbal. Together with the extent of their readership, the influence of books was receding — together, too, with the decline of people's attention span, or with their capacity to concentrate, indeed, to listen. With the increasing propagation of "information" and of "communication" the habits of reading further declined.

I now come to the most difficult of these necessarily generalized and inaccurate summaries of devolution: that of art, which in the Modern Age was inseparable from the ideals not only of beauty but of representation. Much of the art of the Middle Ages was symbolic, and idealized. The Renaissance of course discovered humanism, the beauty of the human body, and the complexity of human nature; and it had begun with an emulation of Greek and Roman art which was marked by "mimesis," or in another word: "re-presentation." A deep shift in consciousness at the end of the eighteenth century then affected art, first of all poetry and painting. This was the conscious recognition of imagination, beyond the older idea of inspiration (an early recognition of the inseparability of the observer from what he observes). During the nineteenth century literature and architecture were increasingly influenced, if not altogether inspired and formed, by historicity. Meanwhile realism and naturalism in poetry and painting were more and more affected by the artist's comprehension of the limitations of "objectivity" — that is, of the entire separation of the observer (and of course of the artist) from his subject. "Impressionism," thus, was no more the mere result of the invention of photography than impressionist music was the result of the invention of the phonograph.

After the early nineteenth century the artist was no longer seen as an artisan, meaning a craftsman, but rather as a person of unusual, indeed, superior sensitivity. By the early twentieth century — even before the catastrophe of World War I — what was oddly, and belatedly, called "modern art" meant a drastic and brutal departure from the traditions and the achievements of the Modern Age. This is no place to expatiate upon, or even to illustrate, this reactionary argument; instead I shall only cite the words of the English poet Philip Larkin: "It seems to me undeniable that up to this century literature used language in the way we all use it, painting represented what anyone with normal vision sees, and music was an affair of nice noises rather than nasty ones. The innovation of 'modernism' in the arts consisted of doing the opposite. I don't know why, I'm not a historian. You have to distinguish between things that seemed odd when they were new but are now quite familiar, such as Ibsen or Wagner, and things that seemed crazy when they were new and seem crazy now, like *Finnegans Wake* and Pound and Picasso." "Crazy" — and ugly: because the ending of the ideals of re-presentation was also marked by an increasing tendency in letters, buildings, music, painting, poetry, to ugliness.

This Jeremiad has its conditions, and limitations. One of them involves the distinction between the passing of the Modern Age and the Decline of the West. Of course almost all of the symptoms of the ending of the Modern (or European; or Bourgeois) Age have been most evident within the so-called Western world. But because of the continued influence of Western habits and institutions and practices all over the globe, not a few differences between the customs of the Western and the non-Western world are now sometimes hardly more than differences in timing. The contrast between a bloodless West and the power of the more primitive peoples of the globe (not to speak of Spengler's Europe/Russia antithesis) may or may not be deepening. We are of course only at the beginning of the first "global" civilization—and only on certain transitory and superficial levels. In any event: the near future, the beginning of an age that will succeed the Modern Age, shows many signs of spreading wider than the Western world.

Another limitation is even more evident. This is a chronological limitation of my Jeremiad, which I must defend, at least to some extent. In almost all of the abovementioned spheres of life the rapid dissolution and the malfunctioning of the institutions and ideals of the Modern Age gathered speed during the twentieth century, and especially during its second half. Is this not too shortsighted a view? Their sources and beginnings and symptoms had appeared earlier; but then those were not what I am writing about. It is hardly arguable that in this, as also in many other respects, the twentieth century was a transitional century (as was a century at the end of the Middle Ages, from about 1450 to 1550)—in every sense, the twentieth was also a short century, lasting from 1914 to 1989, seventy-five years. After that, the collapse of Communism (and of the Russian Empire) did not lead to a conservative reaction: the symptoms of dissolution continued—indeed, many of them gathered speed during the last decade of the chronological twentieth century (no fin-de-siècle then). No, history is not a mechanical clock: the pendulum never swings back. But human events and minds change, though slowly; something different, something new is beginning.

A third limitation consists in the condition that the mutation of characteristics and institutions and habits is especially (though not at all exclusively) evident in the United States and in the industrially or technically most "advanced" countries of the Western world. This should not be surprising: after all, the American historical handicap (as well as the once American advantage) was due to the condition that the institutions of the United States were born in the very middle of the Modern Age, in the century of the so-called Enlightenment, whereby the people of the United States have been less immune to the shortcomings of modernity than other peoples whose mental and physical make-up carries some living memories of older epochs, of an older and different past.[8] After 1989 an unprecedented situation arose: the United States was the only Superpower in the world. Does this connote the Apogee of the Modern Age (the age that had given birth to the United States of America)? Not at all.

And then there is Christianity. Its churches have been emptying. Yet something like this has happened before, and often. (One example: perhaps never in the two thousand years of the Holy See was a Pope as bereft of prestige and power as Pius VI was two hundred years ago, in 1799.) Is Christianity disappearing? I do not think so.

And now: the Contra-Jeremiad. A list of the *enduring* achievements of the Modern Age. Enduring; and lasting; and

---

8. But consider, too, the reciprocal influences of institutions and character. Contrary to accepted views, character influences institutions as much, if not more, than the reverse: and the *character* of most of the American people two hundred years ago was still predominantly Anglo-Celtic, that is, at least to some extent, pre-Enlightenment.

matters still in progress. We are healthier than ever before. (To be more precise: less affected by pain and by contagious illness.) Infant mortality has become minimal. Our life-span has become longer and longer. (Again, most of this progress had taken place in the past 130 years.) Large masses of people are now able to live in conditions of comfort available only to the richest or most powerful of our great-grandparents. Large masses of people drive their own automobiles. Large masses can afford to travel to faraway continents and places in a matter of hours, with enough money to spend. Institutional slavery has largely ceased to exist. Almost every state proclaims itself a democracy, attempting to provide a minimum of welfare to all of its inhabitants. Men have been propelled to the moon and back; they have landed there six times.

We cannot crank our lives backward. We must also know that there were (and are) no Golden Ages of history. The evidences of decay all around us do not mean that there was any ideal period at any time during the Modern Age. In certain fields of life and art and thought: perhaps. In others: certainly not. Yes, it would be pleasant to meet Rembrandt or Bach or Montesquieu or Washington — or perhaps even to live in the age of Edward VII: but only with plenty of money at our disposal, and in at least near-perfect health. Such are illusions amid a then-extant reality of pain and discomfort and illness and other, less tangible but surely prevalent disillusionments.

Moreover, history and life consist of the coexistence of continuity and change. Nothing vanishes entirely. The institutions, the standards, the customs, the habits, the mental inclinations of the Modern Age still exist around us. So does the respect for many of its creative achievements — political, social, but, even more, artistic. (One of them is polyphonic music, which was a unique European creation sometime during the beginning of the era.) The respect for older things has now acquired a tinge of nostalgia — almost certainly part and parcel of the uneasiness with "Progress." During the past forty years the meanings of the adjectives "old" and "old-fashioned" — especially in the United States — have changed from "antiquated" or "outdated" to suggest some things that are reliable, solid, enduring, desirable. This has little to do with "conservatism" or "traditionalism." "Conservatives," especially in the United States, are some of the most strident proponents of "Progress"; their views of the present and the future are not merely shortsighted but laden with a bellowing optimism that is imbecile rather than naive. Nor is the respect for old things simply traditionalist, since a blind obedience to traditional customs marks the mentality and the habits of the most primitive peoples of mankind.

In any event, there is every reason to believe that the respect for (and even the occasional emulation and adaptation of) some of the creations of the Modern Age (surely its achievements in art) will continue and grow. The time will come (if it is not already at hand) when people will look back and respect and admire (perhaps with a sigh, but no matter) — indeed, that they will recognize — the past five hundred years as one of the two greatest eras in the history of mankind, the other having been the "classical" one, Greece and Rome. But here is a difference — and a significant one. The last time something like this happened was five or six hundred years ago, involving but a small minority of people, which is not what is happening now. At that time men began to look back at the achievements and the letters and the art of Greece and Rome, idealizing them, and emulating them. (All art begins with emulation.) That was the Renaissance, a re-birth: the word is telling. It marked the beginning of modern historical consciousness — although that was imperfect and incomplete, because of its almost unrestricted idealization of the Classical Age, of the ancients. Its admirers dismissed the entire Middle Ages, their still then present and their recent past (even though the idea and the term "Middle Ages" did not yet exist). They took their inspiration from *two* ages away, farther back. This is not happening now. Something else is: our respect and admiration for the age that is now past but which existed immediately before our times and which in many ways is still close to us and extant within us. And this is a symptom of the evolution of our historical consciousness which may be acquiring novel forms and which is not weakening.

There are other results of this coexistence of continuity and change — unplanned and unforeseen ones. They are the unexpected consequences of changes in the nature of institutions and in that of accepted ideas — wherein we may detect the, often paradoxical, appearances of dualities.

Again it was Tocqueville who wrote about the inevitable fallibility of all human institutions: when people tend to stretch

or carry their original and particular features to extremes, these
become the very opposites of their original intentions.

Here are a few examples.

At the end of the Modern Age constitutions and courts
have extended lawfulness to private acts of all kinds
(sometimes to the extent of obscenity) — at a time
when fewer and fewer people appreciate or are able to
cultivate privacy.

Large masses of people are able to acquire residences
they legally "own" — when, in reality, they merely rent
them (since they will almost never pay for them in full;
nor do they expect to stay in them for more than a few
years). Permanence of residence, which is one basis of
civilization, is no longer an ideal. Many conditions, including taxation, work against it.

The egalitarian notion of democracy, meaning the lessening of class differences, exists at the same time that
many people are uncomfortable with a classless society
in which they are unable to identify themselves and in
which they depend on paltry and temporary associations.

Legal, or even social, distinctions of race are diminishing, and the rights and privileges of formerly restricted
races are institutionalized and extended — at the same
time that the fear and hostility of races among people
may be growing.

We have already seen that the sums spent on education
have become enormous, and that the time young peo-

ple spend in school amounts to twenty or more years —
at the same time that their knowledge of the world is
deficient, together with their ability to read and write
and to express themselves well.

"Liberals," who, earlier in the Modern Age, had advocated limiting the powers of the state, have throughout
the twentieth century advocated government interven-
tion in many fields, including a guarantee to welfare of
many kinds. "Conservatives," who had once stood for
the defense of traditions, have become chief advocates
of technology and of militarization and even of popu-
lism, all in the name of "Progress."

The power and function of government, its interven-
tions and regulations in more and more spheres of life,
have grown — at the same time that the selective indig-
nation of people about such extensions of "government" goes apace with the decline of the authority and
respect for the state.

The progressive applications of medicine and surgery
and therapy are astounding — at the same time that
more and more people are dependent on medicine and
on medications throughout their adult lives. Here is
one of the greatest, and perhaps deepest, changes toward the end of the Modern Age. In the past most
human illnesses came from the outside: from injuries or
infections of many kinds. By the twentieth century most
illnesses came from the inside of the human being. We
may know their pathogenesis (their symptoms and
their development) but seldom their etiology (their

origin). This means that many of our ailments are, at least to some extent, psychosomatic (just as all of our perceptions are, at least to some extent, extrasensory) — another illustration of the increasing intrusion of mind into matter.

The long-awaited equality of women has been legalized and established and, in many ways, guaranteed — at the same time that the relations, including the most intimate ones, between men and women have become complicated and even brutalized. Many women have gained their "independence" at the cost of increasing loneliness.

The incredible access to "information," again at the end of the Modern Age, obscures the condition that, at the same time, much of that "information" is meaningless; and when many of the purveyors of "information" make it dependent or, worse, subordinate to "entertainment." The ability of great masses to see and visit distant parts of the globe has increased exponentially, not only through pictorial and other "communications" but by the increasing and cheapening opportunities of travel — at the same time that the knowledge of people about other peoples is less substantial and more superficial than before.

The fantastic development of communications at the end of the Modern Age makes it possible for almost everyone to see or speak to people across the world in an instant — at the same time that real communications, meaning the talking and listening of people to each other, including parents and children, husbands and wives, even lovers, has become rarer and rarer — in sum: when personal communications are breaking down.

At the end of the Modern Age the position and the power of the United States is unique; the only Superpower in the world, having achieved such a status through much goodwill and of course good fortune — at the same time that the respect of many people (including many Americans themselves) for the present standards of American civilization and of American popular "culture" decline.

Such a list of paradoxical dualities may be endless. But now we arrive at the greatest and gravest duality — indeed, the greatest and gravest problem looming before us at the end of the Modern Age.

Recall Gibbon's sentence of more than two hundred years ago: barbarism and its catastrophes are now inconceivable "unless the face of nature is changed." Now, for the first time in the history of mankind, dangers and catastrophes of nature are potentially (indeed, here and there actually) threatening nature and humanity together. These dangers are man-made. They include not only horribly destructive atomic and biological weapons but many effects on the nature and on the atmosphere of the globe by the increasing presence and intrusion of the results of applied science. So at the end of the Modern

Age the control and the limitation and even the prohibition of
some of the applications of science—including genetic engineering—becomes a, sometimes global, necessity. At the same
time there exists no international or supra-national (and in
most cases not even a national) authority that would enforce
such measures.

In view of this prospect the confusion and the split-
mindedness characteristic near or at the end of an age appears.
Most "conservatives," votaries of what is still wrongly called
"capitalism" and of technical progress, deny the need to pre-
serve or conserve. Most "liberals" still cling to outdated dogmas
of the so-called Enlightenment, unwilling to question the validity of "Science." This kind of schizophrenia is evident, too,
among the Greens or environmentalists — otherwise an interesting and promising appearance of a movement that, for the first
time in modern history, prefers the conservation of Nature to
the inroads of Finance and Science—since the same "Greens"
who militate in favor of laws and authority to halt the ravages
against nature at the same time militate against laws and author-
ities that still claim to protect families and forbid abortions. The
very word "environmentalism" is inaccurate and even misleading, as if mankind were one thing and its "environment" another. Instead of recognizing their unavoidable coexistence,
many environmentalists are also anti-humanists, wishing to exclude all human traces from their cult of wilderness and wild-
ness. They are unwilling to recognize how one of the finest
achievements of the Modern Age—in its art, in its habitations,
indeed in its civilization—was the gradual formation of landscapes, from which a human presence is not, indeed cannot be,

excluded, since the ideal landscape suggests a harmony between the land and the signs of a habitation therein.

Still, after all, the existence of Greens and of environmentalists is a promising symptom — despite their still present split-mindedness of being anti-conservative and conservative at the same time. At the end of the Modern Age, for the first time in two hundred years, more and more people, in more and more fields of life, have begun to question the still present and now outdated idea of "Progress" — an idea which, in its present form, appeared at the beginning of the Modern Age: an ideal as well as an idea that has now begun to lose at least some of its appeal.

Some time during the past quarter of the twentieth century the word "post-modern" appeared: another symptom of the uneasy sense (rather than a clear recognition) that we are living through (or, rather, facing) the end of an age. The prefix "post-" in itself is telling. There is some sense of historical consciousness in it (as for example in "post-Communist" or "post-impressionist" or "post-liberal"), the prefix "post-" being historical (and spatial), unlike "anti-," which is fixed and mathematical: "post-modern" is not necessarily "anti-modern." Yet the meaning (as different from the sense) of "post-modern" has been and remains inadequate, and worse than imprecise: it is vague, to the extent of being unhistorical. This is not the place to describe or analyze the various offshoots (often hardly more than excrescences) of "post-modernism," such as Structuralism, Deconstructionism, the search for "mentalités," and of their intellectual spokesmen. Yes, behind the employment of the "post-modern" category we can detect the uneasy and long overdue recognition that such fixed categories as Objectivism, Scientism, Realism, Naturalism are now passé — they belonged to a bourgeois world and its era. So often the apostles and acolytes of post-modernism are but another, updated twentieth-century version of "post-," indeed, of *anti*-bourgeois: they are confused excrescences of "modernism." But much of the Modern, or Bourgeois, era had well preceded the twentieth or even the nineteenth century, that apogee of the bourgeois age. Besides, most academics and "post-modernist" intellectuals still shy away from abandoning their faith in the Enlightenment, in the Age of Reason — even though the Age of Reason was inseparable from the rise of the bourgeoisie, and even though most of its spokesmen were bourgeois. And wasn't romanticism, in many ways a reaction to the unalloyed faith in Reason, also part of the Modern Age? "Post-modernism" is anti-rationalist or anti-positivist: but what else is new? The powerful recognition that the acts and the thoughts and the wishes of people, together with their expressions, were and are circumscribed by their historical conditions (whereby "facts" are neither absolute, nor timeless) was pronounced by Burke, two centuries before the convoluted propositions of Parisian or American intellectuals.

There is a difference between "post-modern" intellectualism and "post-modern" art. We have seen that the Modern Age — as we still use that approximate term — began about five hundred years ago; that "modern," too, as the antonym of "ancient" emerged, at least in English, about four hundred years ago. Yet the widespread usage and application of the adjective to life and art, such as "modern woman," "modern design," "modern architecture," "modern art," and so on, appeared mostly in the 1895–1925 period. So: what is "post-modern"? A reaction to the twentieth century? Or to the nineteenth? Or to the eighteenth, seventeenth, sixteenth? A reaction to, or a step ahead from — Picasso? Or Meissonier? Or Poussin? One form of art to which "post-modern" may be applicable is music: but, again, only in a narrow chronological sense. By "modern music" we customarily designate the period beginning from Wagner (or, even better, from Debussy), ending with Poulenc, Ibert, Honegger, Webern, Duruflé — the period recognizably 1880–1950. Is "post-modern" music therefore a reaction to, or a step ahead from not only, say, Strauss but also Gershwin? If so, then only orchestral compositions after about 1950 are "post-modern." In popular music, "modern" was the high period of jazz, approximately 1914–1950, after which "post-modern" is rock, an electronic application of primitivism and barbarism. In architecture "modern," after about 1895, amounted to anti- or non-historical, or to anti- or non-traditional.[9] And "post-modern" architecture either does not exist or it is hardly more than a reaction against Bauhaus and Frank Lloyd Wright and Le Corbusier — but often only in bits of ornamentation and a few other smallish details. As in a few scattered examples in other arts, a reaction to the brutal senselessness of "modern"

9. The main mark of most nineteenth-century architecture was its eclectic borrowing of historical styles. In a (largely Spenglerian) sense this marked the decline of artistic (or "cultural") vitality. In another sense it was also the mark of a spreading historical consciousness.

architecture has produced either further exaggerations of form-
lessness or little more than the partial application of a few historical or traditional esthetic styles here and there. If "post-
modern" architecture and art are nothing more than reactions
to post-1895 modernism, the term is inadequate and imprecise.

Another belated, confused, and imprecise word is the current political-sociological term of "modernization." If it means
anything it is a confused and feeble substitute word for something like Americanization.

Yes, we are at—we are living through—the end of an age.
The best of the "post-modern" thinkers and intellects may sense
this but that is all. What Sheridan said in the House of Com-
mons more than two hundred years ago about another Mem-
ber's speech applied to them perfectly: "[He] said things that
were both true and new; but unfortunately what was true was
not new, and what was new was not true." If "post-modern" has
any proper meaning at all, it should mean an advance to a new
and rising sense of historicity. It ought to amount to a recognition—no matter how weak, incomplete, and sporadic—that
the end of the Modern Age carries within it an oceanic, though
as yet hardly conscious, rise of a new meaning of history, of a
historical consciousness.

We are at the end of an age: but how few people *know* this!
The *sense* of this has begun to appear in the hearts of many; but
it has not yet swum up to the surface of their consciousness.

This will happen, even though there exist many obstacles

to it — among them, enormous but corroding institutions. As these lines are being written, something is happening in the United States that has had no precedent. A great division among the American people has begun — gradually, slowly — to take shape: not between Republicans and Democrats, and not between "conservatives" and "liberals," but between people who are still unthinking believers in technology and in economic determinism and people who are not. The non-believers may or may not be conscious or convinced traditionalists: but they are men and women who have begun not only to question but, here and there, to oppose publicly the increasing pouring of cement over the land, the increasing inflation of automobile traffic of every kind, the increasing acceptance of noisome machinery ruling their lives. Compared with this division the present "debates" about taxes and rates and political campaigns are nothing but ephemeral froth blowing here and there on little waves, atop the great oceanic tides of history.[10] That the present proponents of unending technological "progress" call themselves

10. The current Secretary of the United States Treasury declared that "money" should be "returned" to "the people" so that they could buy "bigger cars and bigger houses." He, and his government, not only are proponents of the "production" of more and more "energy" (instead of its conservation); they are also Cosmocrats, thrusting more and more American rockets and stations into "space." Yet it is at least possible that — just as in the case of the scientists' effort to find the smallest basic particle of the universe (about which see Chapter 3) — our exploration of "space" may be nearing its end. One indication of this is the growing indifference of people to that pursuit. This was already evident more than thirty years ago when the reaction of people to the first American walkers on the moon did not at all compare with the enthusiasm with which they had reacted to Lindbergh's flight across the Atlantic two generations earlier.

"conservatives" is but another example of the degeneration of political and social language.

However — this book is not a political or social pamphlet. Its theme is simple. It has to do with conscious thinking. We have arrived at a stage of history when we must begin thinking about thinking itself. This is something as different from philosophy as it is from psycho-analysis. At the end of an age we must engage in a radical rethinking

of "Progress,"

of history,

of "Science,"

of the limitations of our knowledge,

of our place in the universe.

These are the successive chapters of this book.

TWO

The Presence of Historical Thinking

My vocation. • The historicity of our thinking. • Professional history. • Justice / Truth. • The appetite for history. • History and the novel. • History at the end of a historical age.

When I say that "I am a historian," what does this statement mean? What do people understand by it? Three hundred years ago they would have been unaccustomed to such a designation. Now their first, and most probable, association is: it is this man's occupation. Or, more precisely: it is his professional affiliation. "A historian" — so he is probably employed, in some institution of higher education.[1]

---

1. This kind of association is of course part and parcel of the bureaucratization of entire societies. Yet there are historians who are not thus employed, who are not professors of history. They write history books on their own, which are published. When people know this, their inclination is to identify such a person as an amateur historian; but, more probably, as a *writer.*

There is nothing very wrong with this. A historian who cannot or does not write well cannot be much of a historian; moreover, the historian's instrument is everyday language, dependent on words that are more than the mere packaging of "facts." However, I must recount an amusing, and perhaps not altogether pleasing, experience during a coffee

I do not wish to object to such a professional designation of myself: but it is not entirely to my taste. Yes, early in my life I chose to become a professional historian, to acquire a necessary degree of certification to enable me to seek such employment, to teach in a higher institution of learning, to be admitted into the guild of professional historians, to be recognized as such. All of this has been of course preceded — and succeeded — by something deeper: by an interest in history, but also by my developing sense of a vocation. Interest, inclination, vocation: three overlapping but distinct phases. The consciousness of such a distinction may appear only in retrospect. But that there is a difference, though of course not necessarily an opposition, between a vocation and a professional identification or certification, ought to be obvious.

A sense of vocation, though perhaps rare, is not necessarily good. Fanatics have such a sense; obsessive minds may have such a sense. At the same time a sense of vocation ought to involve at least some self-searching. Very early in my life and in my professional career I began to be interested not only in certain matters of the past about which I wished to know more and more; not only in certain periods of the past, but also in

---

break at a scholarly conference where I had given a paper that was perhaps more fluent and easy than some of the others. I overheard someone answering a question about who I was: "He is a historian; but he is really a writer." There was something slightly deprecatory in this statement. (Such is the professionalization of historianship now in the United States. There are other countries and other languages where, even now, such a statement would not be deprecatory.)

certain problems of their history; in problems of our historical knowledge. The motives of such questioning are almost always mixed and not easily ascertainable. They may not be separable from personal disillusionments and disappointments (in my case from the pretended objectivism in the writings and from the gray ice on the faces of certain professional historians); but, as in everything else, one may know one's purposes better than one's motives. In my life, this led me, perhaps at an unduly early stage of my "professional" career, to think and read and gather material and plan for a work dealing with problems about our very knowledge of history itself, questions including a few novel and radical propositions. They are there in *Historical Consciousness,* a book that took me — with various interruptions — almost thirteen years to complete. It was during my work on the first, often convoluted, draft of *Historical Consciousness* that, sometime in the late summer of 1958, I suddenly found that I might have arrived at what seemed to me an intellectual discovery of considerable magnitude. How this happened and what it meant are related briefly in my *Confessions of an Original Sinner* almost three decades later; and it will be summed up in a paragraph later in this book, in Chapter 4. In any event, that was a crucial stage in my intellectual pilgrimage and in my historical vocation, of which the present book is a short essay-like summa.

However — this book is *not* about myself. It is not autobiographical. Yet these introductory remarks are unavoidable. About this unavoidability I cannot but cite a great Hungarian Catholic poet, János Pilinszky, who wrote how he had been inspired to recognize this condition by reading St. Augustine and Simone Weil: "There are the personal, the non-personal, and the collective areas of life. One cannot reach the non-personal except from what is personal; from the collective, never. Something must become personal first; after that one may go forward to what is no longer personal."

All living beings have their own evolution and their own life-span. But human beings are the only living beings who know that they live while they live—who know, and not only instinctively feel, that they are going to die. Other living beings have an often extraordinary and accurate sense of time. But we have a sense of our history, which amounts to something else. "The *question* of scientific knowledge" is the title and subject of my next chapter; the *presence* of historical thinking is the title and subject of this one. Scientific knowledge, dependent as it is on a scientific method, is by its nature open to question. The existence of historical knowledge, the inevitable presence of the past in our minds, is not. We are all historians by nature, while we are scientists only by choice.

Modern scientific thinking appeared about three or four hundred years ago, together with a then new view of the globe and of the universe. It meant the methodical investigation of nature, and eventually the manipulation of a kind of knowledge which, once applied, changed the world and our lives in unimaginable ways. Eventually Science came to mean (mostly, though not exclusively) the Science of Nature: our knowledge of things and of organisms other than ourselves. At the same time, about three or four hundred years ago, there occurred another evolution, first in Western Europe: a passage from a kind of historical thinking that had existed for a long time to a kind of historical consciousness that was a relatively new phenomenon. Of these two developments the importance of the first, of Science, has of course been recognized—with every reason, given its successive and successful applications; the second, hardly at all. Yet it may be argued that the second, involving man's knowledge of man, may have been—perhaps more and more evidently now—as important, if not more important, than the first.

Shakespeare in *Henry V:* "There is a history in all men's lives." This poetic phrase has a wider meaning in the democratic age, issuing from a recognition that every person is a historical person (and that every source is a historical source).[2] This is—

2. The first edition of the *Dictionary of the French Academy,* published in 1694, defined history as the "narration of actions and of matters worth remembering." The eighth edition, in 1935, said much the same: "the account of acts, of events, of matters worth remembering." *Dignes de mémoire!* Worth remembering! What nonsense this is! Is the historian the kind of person whose training qualifies him to tell ordinary people what is worth remembering, to label, or to authenticate persons or events as if they were fossil fish or pieces of rock? Is there such a thing as a person and another such as a historical person? Every event is a historical event; every source is a historical source; every person is a historical person.

or, rather, should be — obvious. No less obvious is one result of the democratic development of the world. This has been the widening of the nineteenth-century practice of largely political history toward social history, from the history of governments to the history of the governed. (Alas, so many of the proponents and practitioners of the latter have been treating history as a kind of retrospective sociology.) Together with this widening there also have been attempts to deepen the scope and sharpen the focus of historical research. (Alas, so many of the so-called post-modern theoreticians of history have been writing analyses of texts and of statistics employing large quantities of words or numbers in the service of small amounts of thought.)

There is the past; there is the remembered past; there is the recorded past. The past is very large, and it gets larger every minute: we do not and cannot know all of it. Its remnant evidences help: but they, too, are protean and cannot be collected and recorded in their entirety. Thus history is more than the recorded past; it consists of the recorded and the recordable and the remembered past. The past in our minds *is* memory. Human beings cannot create, or even imagine, anything that is entirely new. (The Greek word for "truth," *aletheia,* also means: "not forgetting.") "There is not a vestige of real creativity *de novo* in us," C. S. Lewis once wrote. No one can even imagine an entirely new color; or an entirely new animal; or even a third sex. At best (or worst) one can imagine a new combination of already existing — that is, known to us — colors, or monsters, or sexes. There is a startling and corresponding recognition of this condition in Goethe's *Theory of Colours.* In the Preface of that extraordinary and difficult work he wrote that "strictly speaking, it is useless to attempt to express the nature of a thing abstractedly. . . . We should try in vain to describe a man's character, but let his acts be collected and an idea of the character will be presented to us." And: "As we before expressed the opinion that the history of an individual displays his character, so it may here be well affirmed that the history of science is science itself."[3] This is a prophetic foretelling of Heisenberg and Bohr, who more than one hundred years later were compelled to conclude that the history of quantum theory *is* quantum theory; or that the best way to teach quantum theory is to teach its historical evolution. William James wrote: "You can give humanistic value to almost anything by teaching it historically. Geology, economics, mechanics, are humanities when taught by reference to the successive achievements of the geniuses to whom these sciences owe their being. Not taught thus, literature remains grammar, art a catalogue, history a list of dates, and natural science a sheet of formulas and weights and measures."[4]

In sum, the history of anything amounts to that thing itself. History is not a social science but an unavoidable form of thought. That "we live forward but we can only think backward" is true not only of the present (which is always a fleeting illusion) but of our entire view of the future: for even when we think of the future we do this by *remembering* it. But history cannot tell us anything about the future with certainty. Intelligent research, together with a stab of psychological understanding, may enable us to reconstruct something from the

3. Johann Wolfgang von Goethe, *Theory of Colours,* London, 1840, pp. xvii, xxiv.
4. William James, *Memories and Studies,* New York, 1911, pp. 312–313.

past; still, it cannot help us predict the future. There are many reasons for this unpredictability (for believing Christians let me say that Providence is one); but another (God-ordained) element is that no two human beings have ever been exactly the same. History is real; but it cannot be made to "work," because of its unpredictability. A curious paradox is that while science is abstract, it can be made to work. Abraham Lincoln (or one's grandmother) *really* existed; there was and will be no one exactly like him or like her. But the material elements of Science never exist in perfect or unalloyed form. H_2O is a most useful definition of water; yet of a liquid that, in reality, does not and cannot absolutely exist: we may find, or produce, a distillation of 99.99 percent H_2O but not of 100 percent "purity." Yet because of mechanical causality, scientific knowledge can be put to practical use: to a nearly incredible extent of precision and of predictability it can be made to "work."

One reason for this paradox is the essential difference between mechanical and other historical causalities; that what happens is inseparable from what people think happens. Inseparable: but not identical, and also not enduring. People may be wrong in thinking what happens, and they may have been wrong in thinking what happened. A man thinks that the motor stopped because of the failure of the water pump, whereas it was the oil pump. When he then learns that the real source of the trouble was the oil pump, his realization of the source of the trouble means an increase in the quantity and in the extent of his knowledge. But when it comes to a human event, a later realization that what had happened was not what we thought happened usually involves an increase of the *quality* of our knowledge, together with a decrease of the quantity in our memory. (Something happens to us today, something bothersome, whereof we can remember the smallest details. A few years later we recall that day, having forgotten many of its details; yet we may say to ourselves: "Why was I so upset about that then?" Or: "Why had I not noticed that then?" The quantity of our knowledge of the details of that day has waned; but the quality of our knowledge — and understanding — of what had happened may have increased.)

Human understanding is a matter of quality, not of quantity. At times it is a (sudden, rather than gradual) synthesis of accumulated knowledge. But this happens not often. The purpose of understanding differs from the scientific purpose of certainty, and of accuracy. We also know that human understanding of other human beings is always, and necessarily, imperfect. There are odd and illogical elements in its functioning. One of them is that understanding may precede knowledge, instead of being simply consequent to it. Another is that understanding, too, depends on memory. We often think that a failure, or defect, of memory amounts to an insufficiency of knowledge. Yet there, too, there is some kind of understanding at the bottom of the trouble, since we both understand and know what we wish to recall, except that we cannot yet bring those words or names or numbers up to the surface of our mind clearly. Another example is the inevitable dependence of understanding on comparison and contrast. That contrast is an inevitable element of color, indeed, of the very act of seeing. An early proponent of this inevitable condition was the Renaissance painter, poet, philosopher, musician, architect Alberti. Critical of the categorical "definitions" of philosophers, Leone Battista Alberti wrote *On Painting:* "All knowledge of large, small; long, short; high, low; broad, narrow; clear, dark; light and shadow and every similar attribute is obtained by comparison. . . . All things are known by comparison, for comparison contains within itself a power which immediately demonstrates . . ."[5] And just as our act of seeing depends on contrast, our knowledge of the present depends on our knowledge of the past.

This dependence of understanding on contrast and comparison does not necessarily mean the relativity of all human knowledge. "But where would we be if we could speak only of things we know with certainty?" asked the sixteenth-century French historian Henri Voisin de La Popelinière — who nonetheless proposed the necessity of advancing to a "complete" history, including much besides the recorded acts and discourses of rulers.[6] Four hundred years later the solitary Russian thinker

5. Cited in Nancy C. Struever, *The Language of History in the Renaissance,* Princeton, 1970, p. 51. Also ibid., p. 70: Alberti's friend, Coluccio Salutati: "Eloquence is difficult, but history is even more difficult."
6. "L'histoire digne de ce nom doit estre generale." From George Huppert, *The Idea of Perfect History: Historical Erudition and Historical Philosophy in Renaissance France,* Urbana, Illinois, 1970. A very impressive work, proving what I overlooked in *Historical Consciousness,* where I situated the crystallization of modern historical consciousness largely in the seventeenth century, not earlier. (Huppert, p. 182: "In sum, then, the French prelude to modern historiography was more than a prelude, it was a stunning first act, full of consequences.") P. 166: "Here then is historical-mindedness — historicism, if you will — solidly established in the mental habits of a handful of scholars in the sixteenth century. Neither Locke's psychology nor the scientific revolution seem to have been prerequisites for the growth of a sense of history as we understand it. This state of mind existed in all of its

Mikhail Bakhtin wrote that neither human understanding nor creative thinking is the result of a synthesis. "On the contrary, it consists in the intensification of one's own *distinctness* from others; it consists in fully exploiting the privilege of one's own unique place outside other human beings." This is not solipsism, not subjectivism, and not even relativism. "This outsidedness must be preserved if solidarity with others is to be fruitful. . . . Our empathy with others [must be] completed with elements of our own perspective. Sympathetic understanding is not a mirroring, but a fundamentally and essentially new valuation, a utilization of my own architectonic position in being outside another's inner place."[7] Outside, yes: but with the intention to understand the other one, to participate, even if to a necessarily incomplete extent. Of course: love is always the love of *another*.[8]

---

essentials before 1660. It disappeared again — or at least it was weakened and suppressed — in the course of the next century, precisely during the time when science and Cartesian rationalism became important features of European culture." It was more than a historical oddity.

7. Aileen Kelly, *View From the Other Shore,* New Haven, 1999, p. 210.

8. Consider what happens when we are concerned or worried about someone who is dear to us. Can we separate our concerns for her from how that concern affects (and will affect) us? There *may* be an imbalance of these two concerns; between our thinking *mostly* about her and our thinking *mostly* about how her situation affects or will affect us. But *in any case,* these concerns are inseparable: both "objectivity" (an exclusive concentration only on her condition) and "subjectivity" (an exclusive concentration only on my condition) are impossible. Our consciousness and our knowledge (and our concern and our expectations) are participatory, and thus inseparable.

Simone Weil: "I used to believe, with regard to any problem what-

But perhaps the most important element of historical thinking is the understanding that our knowledge of history (indeed,
our entire knowledge of the past; indeed, even our personal
memory) is not and cannot be restricted to "what actually happened," since potentiality is inherent in actuality. This is true of
"great" historical events as well as of intimate human situations,
because human inclinations, even when they do not mature into
definite acts, are essentially potential signs of actualities. As
Johan Huizinga wrote: "The sociologist, etc., deals with his
material as if the outcome were given in the known facts:
he simply searches for the way in which the result was already determined in the facts. The historian, on the other hand,
must always maintain towards his subject an indeterminist
point of view. He must constantly put himself at a point in the
past at which the known factors still seem to permit different
outcomes. If he speaks of Salamis, then it must be as if the
Persians might still win . . . "9

The relationship of potentiality and actuality correspond to
the difference — again, a qualitative as much as a quantitative

---

ever, that to know was to solve the problem; now I realize that it means to
know how the problem concerns me."

9. Johan Huizinga, *The Idea of History*. I chose this passage for the epi-
graph, and motto, of one of my books, *The Duel*. The relative success of
this book (1990) and of the related *Five Days in London: 24–28 May 1940*
(1999), is, I am convinced, largely due to the fascination of readers in
reading how close Hitler came at that time to winning the war, and how
Churchill was able to deflect him: in other words, in reading of the existence of a potentiality inherent in, and inseparable from, the actuality of
those times.

difference — between what is significant and what is important. Here is the essential difference between historical and legal evidence — or between historical and legal thinking. Law (at least in a state governed by a constitution) can deal only with actuality, not with potentiality. "The law is a coarse net; and truth is a slippery fish." Yes: but the purpose of law has nothing to do with truth; it is the establishment of justice. Truth and justice are not the same things, even though the pursuit of truth and the pursuit of justice may, on occasion, overlap. But besides the question (or, rather, the obvious primacy) of truth over justice, there are other important differences between historical and legal evidences and thinking. One is that law, after all — inevitably and necessarily — is a closed system, within its own definite rules and regulations. For instance, it does not and should not allow multiple jeopardy: a case, when and if properly tried, is decided once and for all. History (and our memory) is open and never closed; it specializes in multiple jeopardy: its subjects and people are rethought over and over again, and not even necessarily on the basis of newly found evidence. There may be five hundred biographies of Lincoln, but there is hardly reason to doubt that sooner or later there will be a 501st one with something new in its contents, and not necessarily because of new materials that its author has found, but because of a new viewpoint. Another great difference — I am again referring principally to Anglo-American law — is the one between motives and purposes. These two are regrettably confused because of the vocabulary and the practices of twentieth-century psychology and thought, the attribution of motive having become a pestilential intellectual habit.[10] But we must distinguish between the two. Motives come from the past; purposes involve the pull of the future. At its best, Anglo-American law will admit only a "motive" which has been, in one way or another, expressed; in other words, an actuality, not a potentiality. (As Dr. Johnson said: "Intentions must be gathered from acts.") At its worst, unexpressed motives are sometimes attributed and accepted in some courts on the basis of psychological characterization or other dubious "expertise." A proper comprehension of the essential difference between motives and purposes is an essential condition of the pursuit and of the protection of justice and of truth — and of all historical thinking and speaking and writing.

Historical thinking accords with the recognition that human knowledge is neither objective nor subjective but personal and participant. Consciousness (*conscientia*) is participant knowledge. Nearly four hundred years ago Descartes argued, in his *Discourse on Method*, that the study of history was wasteful because we cannot acquire any accurate or certain knowledge of the human past, as we can of mathematics and of the world of nature. Yet another century after Descartes, Vico "said just the opposite. His claim was that the principles of human society, the 'civil world' as he calls it, are actually more certain than the principles governing the natural world, because civil society is a

---

10. One characteristic of Christianity is the condition that it says little about the *motives* of evil, while it says plenty about how evil exists and comes into existence.

human creation"[11] — to which let me add that "the natural world," too, is inseparable from our knowledge of it — for us.

The professionalization of history — or in other words: the certification of historianship — has brought about great, widespread, and fruitful results during the past two hundred years, and especially during the nineteenth century. Still . . . some of the finest historians of the past two hundred years did not have professional degrees. (You can be a poet without having a Ph.D. in Poetry, and, yes, you can be a historian without having a Ph.D. in History.) A problem for most professional historians is that their certification and their craft and their methods are still bound to the practices (and often to the philosophy) of historianship established in the nineteenth century, even though during the twentieth century great changes occurred in the structures of states and societies, together with changes in what I call the structure of events. Except here and there, most historians have been unwilling or unable to adjust the requirements of their craft to these changes. This is understandable (even when it is less justifiable) because of personal reasons, ranging from the conformism of an intellectual bureaucrat to the respectable seriousness of a traditional craftsman. Many of us have met many a "historian" whose main interest seems to be not the study of history but his historianship, meaning his

11. Peter Burke, *Vico,* Oxford, 1985, p. 78.

standing within the profession — a failure in character. Yet we have also met many other historians whose interest and work in history is impervious to fads — small triumphs of character. More important: many of the methods and practices of research and management of sources established by the great historians of the nineteenth century are still valid. But before I turn to some of the problems with "sources," let me make bold to suggest something that more and more professional historians uneasily sense, even though they may be reluctant to state it: that behind the problem of "sources" looms the obvious recognition that documents do not by themselves "make" history; rather, it is history that makes documents. For history is, and always was, something more than a study of records; and just as actuality must, by necessity, include at least a recognition of the element of potentiality, if history is the memory of mankind (which it is), then it is something more than the recorded past; it must include something of the remembered past, too.

That a new structure of society involves new perspectives Tocqueville saw almost 180 years ago. He saw the forest from the trees with an astonishingly clear and acute eye. There is a small chapter, consisting of forty-eight sentences, in the second volume of *Democracy in America,* "Some Characteristics of Historians in Democratic Times," that ought to be read and reread by every historian. (And Tocqueville also practiced what he preached: these generalizations in *Democracy in America* [which was not a history] became, here and there, incarnated in his own history writing twenty years later, in *The Old Regime and the French Revolution.*) The great clear insight of Alexis the Forester was his recognition that above and beyond the

Ancient-Middle-Modern periodization of history in the West rose the present transformation of entire societies into democracies: the passage from the aristocratic to the democratic age; from peoples ruled by minorities to peoples ruled by majorities (even though that is not entirely identical with peoples ruling *themselves*). And it is because of this evolving democratization of the world that some of the problems of modern historical research — and writing — have arisen. I can only sum up some of them inadequately and briefly.

There is the problem of the quantity of materials with which the historian must deal. The nineteenth-century ideal — in many ways, still current — was that of definiteness and completion, meaning the filling of particular gaps in history (more precisely: in our professional historical knowledge) properly and perfectly, in accordance with the accepted norms and methods of the profession. There was (and there still is) merit in this ideal of history being something like the building of a vast and impressive cathedral, to which its professional workmen contribute by adding small pillars here and there, including the filling of small gaps with one brick, if needed, as for example with dissertations or monographs of minor scope. Yet we must keep in mind that no cathedral is ever completed; that repairs and restructurings are needed from to time to time; that the very surroundings of the cathedral change; and that every generation will see the cathedral in new and different ways. And perhaps even more important is the condition that even a great cathedral does not a city make; that with the onset of democracy we have, by necessity, extended the scope of history, so far as its themes and topics go, to the lives (and records) of all kinds of people; so far as its "methods"[12] go, beyond the official archives. History *does* depend on records, but it is not merely a matter of records. And the quantity (and the scope) of materials with which the modern historian deals is greater than ever before. The ideal that, at least concerning a small topic, the historian can — and must — have read everything written about it, exhausting all of the "sources," in many cases is no longer possible, or even reasonably expectable. And then there is the other problem, related to quantity. Democracy, almost invariably, leads to inflation: inflation in the number of people, inflation of papers, inflation of bureaucracy, inflation of records. One hundred years ago it was at least approximately (though not completely) possible for a historian to have read almost all the papers and documentary evidence written to and by and about a political or literary figure. This is no longer so. A "definite" history is necessarily an exaggeration; and an "orthodox" history is necessarily a contradiction in terms.

This oceanic rise in the quantity of potentially useful materials for the historian is of course inseparable from the problem of their quality. (When there is more and more of something, it is worth less and less.) But that is not all. The quality of every document, of every record, indeed of every kind of human expression, depends on its authenticity. With the oceanic tide of

12. The great German historian Theodor Mommsen, more than one hundred years ago: "History is one of those academic subjects which cannot be directly acquired through precept and learning. For that, history is in some measure too easy and in some measure too difficult. The elements of the historical discipline cannot be learned, for every man is endowed with them." The great Jacob Burckhardt, one hundred years ago: history has no method, except one: *bisogna saper leggere* — you must know how to read.

documents — the combined results of spreading democracy, spreading technology, spreading bureaucracy — the authenticity of "sources" with which the historian must deal decreases; in some cases it even disappears. The nineteenth-century canonical rule regarding historical evidence, the essential distinction between "primary" (that is, direct) and "secondary" (that is, successive and indirect) sources is being washed away. Through telephone, teletype, FAX, e-mail, and so on, many statements are unreconstructable, unrecorded, disappearing fast. We also have important documents — for example, letters by Presidents (and not only speeches by speechwriters and other expressions) — that were not only not written but not even dictated or read by them or signed by their own hand. There are records of twentieth-century presidential cabinet sessions that are less authentic than a postcard from one's grandmother found in an old drawer: no matter how mundane are the few words on that postcard, its authenticity exists because of that spiky handwriting, the old stamp and postmark, the yellowed cardboard, its musty smell.

This drastic mutation in the very essence of historical records has its special dangers. The recently fashionable practice of social history does not confront them, at least as long as it is sociological rather than sociographical, which is, alas, often the case.[13] The bringing up of records and statistics of all kinds from distant pasts present another kind of danger: as far as the records go, the danger is not so much their authenticity as their

13. Sociological: scientific, pretending to be *definitive*. Sociographical: *descriptive*, with an appeal to our retrospective and imaginative understanding.

incompleteness; as far as statistics go, the danger exists in the difficulty—at times, impossibility—of ascertaining their correctness. Sooner or later a historian with an independent mind ought to compose a guidebook: "New Problems of Historical Research", a list of warnings about new particular problems. I can mention only a general one. Many of the present "schools" of social history depend on the concept of Economic Man, from the—at times veiled—"scientific" belief that the basic realities of human existence and of historic life and development are material, whereof the mores and morals and thoughts and beliefs of most people are the superstructures. My belief, from an early time in my life, has been the opposite: that (perhaps especially in the democratic age and in democratic societies) the most important matter is what people think and believe—and that the entire material organization of society, ranging from superficial fashions to their material acquisitions and to their institutions—are the consequences thereof.

At the beginning of the twenty-first century, at the very end of the Modern Age, many professional historians seem to agree that historical "objectivity" and historical "determinism" are no longer sacrosanct, indeed, that they are questionable. Yet for many of them this means little more than the mere nodding of heads otherwise preoccupied, since they keep writing and teaching as if history were still determined. The fad for "psychohistory" in the 1960s, the "post-modern" definitions of conditions of "discourse," and the recent tendency among French historians to write about "mentalités" seldom amount, alas, to more than an uneasy feeling of progress along the dusty shoulders of a great roadway on which many stones had broken through the old rutted surface, making the marching a bit uncomfortable (not to speak of the heavy motorized traffic on it). A learned Hungarian thinker and unequaled master of literary history, Antal Szerb (he was murdered in 1944, in the same year as the great French historian Marc Bloch), wrote in his *Introduction to the History of Hungarian Literature* (1934) two prophetic and radiant sentences: "The new science of psychology is still in its infancy, so much so that for an auxiliary science it is nearly useless. In that field the writer of literary history remains alone, bereft of assistance; what he may try could be, at best, an attempt toward a new kind of knowledge that would consist of the study of the historical developments of spiritual and mental structures; perhaps one day that will be called spiritual history — that is, once it appears." Two sentences worth more than many of the volumes nowadays laboriously composed by proponents of psychohistory or of sociological history.

One very random illustration of the disinclination of otherwise well-meaning and thorough and serious historians to consider the personal and participant conditions — and responsibilities — of knowledge I recently found in an otherwise excellent large book by Heinz Huerten, *Deutsche Katholiken, 1918–1945*, which goes beyond the necessarily narrow framework of ecclesiastical history. In his chapter "The German Catholic Church and the murder of the Jews," in which Huerten introduces the problematic question whether German Catholics, priests and bishops, have been true to their faith during the Third Reich, he writes: "Since their decisions were essentially personal ones, they cannot be ultimately criticized by science, and even less can they be offered scientifically." Even keeping in mind that the German word "Wissenschaft," meaning "science" and "knowledge," is broader than the English "science," and with all respect for Huerten's sincerity, such a separation of the "personal" from the "scientific" is inadequate, insufficient.

To ignore the unavoidable personal — and participatory — element of human and historical knowledge is of course the great failure of Objectivism. But there is another (and, in many of its instances, post-modern) danger, when the recognition of the shortcomings of historical Objectivism results in Subjectivism. This is the case of (the once Marxist) E. H. Carr's *What Is History?* (1961). Carr's central argument is that "before you study the history, study the historian," and "before you study the historian, study his historical and social environment." This is a half-truth. The recognition that different persons see the past (and also the present) differently, and that thus every historian is different, does not mean that because he is the product of his past he cannot do otherwise. How about the sons of rich parents who chose to become Marxist? Or — how about former Marxists who chose to become neo-conservatives?[14] Carr's argument is noth-

14. Carr's is a twentieth-century, an automobile-age version of Tolstoy's nineteenth-century nonsense of History as a Locomotive. Both Tolstoy and Carr deny free will. Moreover, the important thing is where the driver is going and not, as Tolstoy declared, the mechanism of the locomotive;

ing but a subjective form of determinism denying not only free will but hopelessly confusing motives and purposes.[15]

This kind of subjectivism is also inherent in the neo-idealist R. G. Collingwood. Recognizing that a German historian who was born in 1900 would see the past differently from a French historian who was born in 1800, Collingwood concluded, "There is no point in asking which was the right point of view. Each was the only one possible for the man who adopted it." *The only one possible?* This is determinism — subjectivist determinism — again. That French historian in 1800 could have been a monarchist, or a republican, or a Bonapartist; that German historian could have been an imperialist or a liberal.[16] That would influence (influence, not determine) their perspectives of the past as well. (To carry this further: the French historian in 1800 could be a Germanophile or a Germanophobe; the German historian in 1900 a Francophobe or a Francophile.

the important question is "What is Carr driving at?" and not "What make is this Carr?"

15. Besides, Carr cannot quite detach himself from the terminology of Objectivity. "It does not follow," he writes, "that, because a mountain appears to take on different angles of vision, it has objectively no shape at all or an infinity of shapes." But the more objective our concept of the shape of the mountain, the more abstract that mountain becomes. For the existence of the mountain was meaningless until men appeared on the scene, and saw it, and eventually called it a mountain. (Much later they conceived it as an objective fact.) Ortega y Gasset in *The Modern Theme* (1923): "Perspective is one of the components of reality. Far from being its deformation it is its organization. A reality which would remain always the same when seen from different points is an absurdity."

16. People do not *have* ideas. They *choose* them. See Chapter 3, pp. 88, 141–142; also p. 185.

That could even affect the choice of their interests: it is at least imaginable that a German historian in 1900 could prefer to read and write about Louis XV and a French historian in 1800 about Frederick William I.)

It is here that the twentieth-century subjectivists, from the early Croce to Becker and Beard and many of the "postmoderns," slid into error. They could not liberate themselves from the scientific worldview, from Descartes's world divided into subjects and objects and from Newton's world where causes always and inevitably precede effects, and where the present is always the product of the past. They went wrong not because they were attacking the illusion of objectivity; they went wrong because, like the objectivists, they were thinking in terms of direct causes, of men as products. Thus subjectivism is also inherent in the neo-idealists Collingwood and Oakeshott, whose otherwise valuable recognitions of the errors of objectivism and materialism and positivism have moved them toward the morass of a merely philosophical — that is, abstract — idealism that is essentially subjectivist.[17]

However — the purpose of this subchapter is not philosophical; it is, rather, a reminder for historians of some things that are real. Such recognitions of reality are inseparable from the knowledge of our own limitations, including the limitations of our profession, of our methods, of our craft. As in all human thought, in history these include the limitations of language. Historians must constantly keep in mind that the instruments

17. See below, Chapter 3, p. 142.

of their craft (and of course of all their thinking) are words, because we think and teach and write with words. It is not only that memory is the womb of the human psyche, and that the Muses were the daughters of Memory: Mnemosyne. The sudden development of speech in children is indeed mysterious, because words are the fundamental signs and symbols of emerging consciousness. They are more than abstract symbols, or units of communication; they are symbols not of *things* but of *meanings* — not of something merely physical but essentially of something mental. Meaning always has an element of revelation in it (whence "literal" vs. "symbolic" meaning is a false distinction). And language exists, grows, and fades together with memory.[18]

Language is not perfect. It exists to communicate, but only what it can communicate. Some things it communicates badly. At the same time the language which can easily make the finest and most numerous distinctions of meaning is the best one. The great danger during our present passage from a verbal to visual "culture" is latent in the impoverishment of language. But language still contains an element of mystery within it: the mystery which is inherent in every human volition, in every human act,

18. The fine Hungarian writer Dezső Kosztolányi (about the absurdity of an international language): "Knife. Yes, someone may tell me that *couteau, coltello, Messer* do not quite correspond to 'knife.' But no one can tell me that knife is not a knife." Confucius: "When words lose their meaning people lose their freedom" — very true. (Yet in Chinese "country," "state," "nation" are one word . . .)

and which too is in essence a matter of quality.[19] And the quality of every human expression depends not only on one's choice of words but also on the intention of the expression and on its historical circumstances. This corresponds to the, alas, overdue recognition that ideas do not exist apart from the men and women who choose to represent and express them — and *when*.

Yes: historical circumstances — because the meaning of every human expression (and hence the meaning of every idea) is inseparable from not only how and where and to whom it is stated but *when:* conditions of historicity that are inseparable from and inherent in the speaker's or writer's intention. Here are two examples. "There are Communists who are murderers." Imagine a Pole or a Russian, say, in 1948, standing up and saying this in Warsaw or Minsk, at a public meeting ruled by Stalinist bureaucrats and chaired by a Communist government minister. Now imagine the same words shouted at a meeting of Young Republicans in, say, Chicago, 1952. Or: "A German Jew is at least as good as a Viennese Nazi." Imagine a German man or woman saying this loudly in a crowded Berlin trolleycar in 1942, as he sees a Jewish man pushed off the platform by an S.S. man bellowing with an Austrian accent. Now imagine the same

19. Owen Chadwick, in *Catholicism and History: The Opening of the Vatican Archives,* Cambridge, 1978, p. 2: "Modern history is sometimes called loosely 'scientific history.'" P. 44: "All historical events remain in part mysterious."

words pronounced in New York before an audience of liberals and emigrés. The differences exist not only in the qualities of courage of the first speakers; and not only because they were directed to different people. I am inclined to think that in the given (that is, historical) circumstances somehow the first statements were *truer* than the second ones: more precisely, they came *closer* to the truth, because they were more remarkable statements in the pursuit of truth, in the midst of the ugly presence and prevalence of accepted untruths. They rang with a higher quality of truth.

Justice is of a lower order than is truth, and untruth is lower than is injustice. The administration of justice, even with the best intentions of correcting injustice, may often have to ignore or overlook untruths during the judicial process. We live and are capable of living with many injustices, with many shortcomings of justice; but what is a deeper and moral shortcoming is a self-willed choice to live with untruths. (All of the parables of Christ taught us to believe in truth, not in justice.) There is no need to expatiate upon this further, except that the difference between the propagation of justice and that of truth, resulting in the difference of the prevalence of injustice and of untruth, has perhaps never been as extensive (and startling) as it is now, at the end of the Modern Age, and in the midst of our democratic age. There may be less injustice — surely of institutionalized injustice — now than ever before. The governments of many states and all kinds of legal establishments profess to dedicate themselves to the elimination of injustice: slavery, exploitation, racial and economic and social discriminations. At least superficially these practices seem to have diminished throughout the world. At the same time there hangs over the world an enormous and spreading dark cloud cover of untruths—especially in this democratic age of mass and "electronic" communications (more often than not aimed at the lowest common denominator of their recipients). And amid this often suffocating discrepancy, which is replete with the gravest of potential dangers, few are aware that the indiscriminate pursuit of justice may turn to insane lengths—indeed, that it may lay the world to waste. (Consider but some of the inhuman techniques of modern war; or the puritanical character and fate of Captain Ahab in *Moby-Dick.*)

We have seen, earlier in this chapter, that there is a difference between historical and legal evidence. But: does the historian know what *is* truth? No, he does not; yet he ought to do better than Pontius Pilate (whom I, for one, could never contemplate without at least a modicum of sympathy). When Pilate asked: "What is truth?" he also implied: "What is untruth?" The historian ought to go one better than that. He ought to see untruth for what it is. His work, really, consists of the pursuit of truth (where Pilate had stopped), often through a jungle of untruths, bushes and weeds and thickets, small and large.

But it is not as simple as that. The pursuit of truth (and the often consequent belief, "Eureka! I found it!") is also historical—meaning that it changes through the ages. There was a time when an avowal of certain truths of faith amounted to a proof of one's belonging to a real community (or the reverse).

This was followed by the so-called Age of Reason, when the assertion of a scientific truth became independent of any other belief (wrongly so). Yes: for God-believers Truth is God / God is Truth, which means: God is eternal. Truth is eternal. But we are not Gods but historical beings, and the fallible descendants of Adam. This has been beautifully expressed by the American Christian thinker Caryl Johnston: "There is, inescapably, an historical dimension in any truthtelling. . . . It is not that 'history' tells the truth (or disguises or determines the truth) as it is that we are ineluctably involved with history in any attempt to tell the truth." Note: *to tell the truth.*[20]

We cannot avoid the historicity of our thinking. As Owen Barfield wrote: "One way or another, what matters is our coming to realize that the way we habitually think and perceive is not the only possible way, not even a way that has been going on very long. It is the way we have *come* to think, the way we have *come* to perceive. Habit is the end product of repeated action in the past, of prolonged behavior in the past. This is as true of mental habit as of any other. And so, if men have at last become incapable of seeing what they once saw, it is because they have gone for so long a time not looking at it."[21]

20. Are we ineluctably involved with history in *thinking* the truth? Yes, because thinking, "cognition," is almost always the result of re-cognition. But all of us experience occasional and mysterious stabs of truth that are *more* than recognitions.
21. Owen Barfield, *History, Guilt, and Habit,* Wesleyan University Press, 1979, p. 74. I consider this — so often hardly recognized — English writer (1898–1998) as one of the greatest, and surely one of the profoundest and clearest (a rare combination!) thinkers in the twentieth century. I am not

But the historicity of our seeing and speaking does *not* amount to the relativity of truth. What history gives a mind, at best, is not a dose of relativism; it gives us certain standards, the power to contrast, and the right to estimate. The belief that truth is relative is no longer the assertion merely of cynics or skeptics but of post-modern philosophers, according to whom there were and are no truths, only modes of discourse, structures of thought and of text. Their relativization of truth is absolute. And yet: truths exist. Their existence, unlike the existence of ideas, is not a matter of our choice. But we are responsible for how, and where, and why, and when we try to express them.

"Facts"—inevitably dependent on their associations and, more important, on their statements (about which see the next chapter)—are not truths. Their statements or expressions can come close to truths—which is the best we can expect. A "fact" is never absolute. Nor is it given to us to fix, to nail down, to state unalterably an absolute truth. We may think that our *concept* (or *idea*) of truth is absolute; yet that, too, only hearkens toward the absolute. (Our very language reflects this. "This is true" is not quite the same as: "This is *the* truth.")

Pascal: "Truth is so subtle a point that our instruments are too blunt to touch it exactly. When they do reach it, they crush the point and bear down around it, more on the false than on the true." Kierkegaard: "The pure truth is for God alone. What is given to us is the pursuit of truth." This is not relativism. (If

---

alone in this. So had his friend C. S. Lewis considered Barfield (also T. S. Eliot at least on one occasion).

truth does not really exist, indeed, if it is wholly relative: why pursue it at all?) And for believers, the sense that truths exist ought to be strengthened by the cognition (or consciousness) that the pure truth is for God alone — an existence that is independent of us and yet the potential sense of which is within us.

A little more than a century ago the English historian Lord Acton claimed that historical science had reached a stage when a history of the Battle of Waterloo could be written that would not only be perfectly acceptable to French and British and Dutch and Prussian historians but would be unchanging, perennial, and fixed. Already Acton's great contemporary John Cardinal Newman said that Acton "seems to me to expect more from History than History can furnish." And a century later we have (or at least ought to have) a more chastened and realistic perspective. Acton believed that history (very much including the history of the Church) was a supremely important matter — yes — and that the purpose of history is the definite, and final, establishment of truth — no. Just as the purpose of medicine is not perfect health but the struggle against illness, just as the purpose of law is not perfect justice but the pursuit of it through the vigilance against injustice, the purpose of the historian is not the establishment of perfect truth but the pursuit of truth through a reduction of ignorance, including untruths.

There are many historians who would not find such a statement sufficiently satisfactory. They are not to be blamed for this, nor are they to be blamed for a condition which is much larger than their own profession: the intellectual and mental and spiritual crisis at the end of the Modern Age, of which the bureaucratization of intellectual professions, including historianship, is but a consequence. But they ought to be blamed for their ignorance of (or lack of interest in) an amazing condition: the relatively recent development of a spreading appetite for history in the world, something that exists contrary to so many other superficial symptoms. For this happens at a time when many people know *less* history than their parents or grandparents had known; but when *more* people are interested in history than ever before. On the one hand, less history is being required and taught in schools than earlier in the twentieth century. On the other hand there exists an appetite for history throughout the world — and perhaps particularly in the United States — that has no precedents.[22] There are so many evidences of this that I can list only a few. There are history programs and history channels on television, historical films, historical "documentaries" and "docudramas," obviously responding to the interests of millions, dealing with topics that were hardly featured as late as two generations ago. There exist popular historical magazines, with a widespread readership. There are three times

22. This widespread appetite for history exists when no such widespread appetite for science exists. Yet it is science that has produced its most wondrous and hardly imaginable applications during the twentieth century. In the 1920s Henry Ford declared, "History is bunk," and Herbert Hoover's Secretary of Commerce said: "Tradition is the enemy of progress." No "conservatives" or even "liberals" think that way now.

as many local historical societies in the United States as there were sixty years ago: their membership includes many younger people, not only old ladies in tennis shoes whose interests are primarily genealogical.

Of course the historical appetite of people is served, and will continue to be served, with plenty of junk food. Of that professional historians may be aware. Yet the existence of this appetite for history is ignored by many of them — and, alas, by most administrators of educational institutions.

Perhaps the most startling evidence of this appetite — perhaps more precisely: of this recent evolution of consciousness — has been the (now at least fifty-year-old) change in the relationship between history and the novel. Within commercial publishing, popular histories have been outselling novels for at least fifty years. It is now accepted that serious biographies belong to history: biographies sell quite well, while the very methods of serious biographers have become historical. Interest in history and interest in the novel developed together about 250 years ago; they were part and parcel of the then evolving historical consciousness. That was a new phenomenon, since the novel as such hardly existed before that. The novel was not really a new version of epic in prose. It described people and events who were not mythical but real, with whom people could identify themselves in one way or another.

Then arose the historical novel, in the nineteenth century, when writers recognized that they could create more interesting stories against a rich historical background. But during the twentieth century a reverse development occurred. More and more it was not the novel that absorbed history but it was history that began to absorb the novel. So far as readership goes, we have seen that the appetite for all kinds of readers for history and for biography has risen at the same time that their appetite and interest for novels has decreased. But — significantly — more and more writers began to sense this (even as they have not recognized its meaning), experimenting with new hybrid genres that are the opposites of the old historical novel, since in their confections history is not the background but the foreground. One manifestation of this is the new hybrid thing that has the silly name of "faction."[23]

"Our time is emerging as a golden age of American history and biography," writes the excellent historian of California, Kevin Starr. "As the American novel, in fact, has become more

23. "All kinds of writers have been trying this (Upton Sinclair, Dos Passos, Irwin Shaw, Styron, Doctorow, Mailer, Sontag, De Lillo, Vidal, Pynchon in this country, many others abroad . . .). What is significant is that these novelists are, all, interested in history. What they have been doing is the reverse of the historical novel, where history was the colorful background. For these twentieth-century novelists history is the foreground, since it attracts them. But most of these authors don't really know that, which is why their works are flawed: for they illegitimately, and sometimes dishonestly, mix up history and fiction. So they include and twist and deform and attribute thoughts and words and acts to historical figures — Lincoln, Wilson, Roosevelt, Kennedy — who actually existed. That is illegitimate, since it produces untruths — no matter that some academic historians may say it serves salutary purposes, as it introduces all kinds of people to history, after all. They are wrong. What they ought to recognize, rather, is the untrammeled spreading of a historical consciousness whereby it is indeed possible that in the future the novel may be entirely absorbed by history, rather than the contrary." From the Introduction of my *A Thread of Years* (1998).

narrow, more internal and fragmented, more solipsistic in its inability to grasp and refract social dynamics in the manner of its [previous] masters . . . American historians and biographers have come to the fore as the providers of imaginative as well as social scientific interpretation."[24] This may be especially true of biography. During the nineteenth century many professional historians, due to the largely German-inspired canons of their craft, eschewed biography. In this respect the English tradition was an exception, with enduring and widening results especially during the second half of the twentieth century (one of the few promising signs at a time of intellectual decay), to the extent that the appetite of the reading public for serious biographies is now larger than ever before, and that every serious biographer now follows the process of historical research.

Meanwhile two directions of the novel have become discernible: one tendency increasingly toward poetry, the other — more widespread and more important — toward history: and there is at least some reason to believe that sooner or later history may absorb the narrative novel almost entirely. New kinds of historical literature will of course appear — they are already appearing — including some very questionable ones. But Carlyle was probably right when we wrote, "In the right interpretation of History and Reality does genuine poetry lie." Or Maupassant (in his preface to *Pierre et Jean*): "The aim of the

24. In Kevin Starr's review of a biography of Randolph Hearst (by David Nasaw, in the *Los Angeles Times Book Review*, 18 June 2000) — which I read on the very day when I first composed these pages. "Coincidences are spiritual puns . . ."

realistic novelist is not to tell a story; to amuse us or to appeal to our feelings, but to compel us to reflect, and to understand the darker and deeper meaning of events."[25] A historian could have written that.

More than one hundred years ago Thomas Hardy wrote:

> Conscientious fiction alone it is which can excite
> a reflecting and thoughtful and abiding interest
> in the minds of thoughtful readers of mature age,
> who are weary of puerile inventions and famish-
> ing for accuracy; who consider that in representa-
> tions of the world, the passions ought to be
> proportioned as in the world itself. This is the in-
> terest which was excited in the minds of the
> Athenians by their immortal tragedies, and in the
> minds of Londoners at the first performances of
> the finer plays of three hundred years ago.[26]

I am convinced that *conscientious history* is now replacing that desideratum which Hardy stated as *conscientious fiction*. It is history which can excite a reflecting and abiding interest in the minds of thoughtful readers of mature age, who are weary (and

25. János Pilinszky: "The novel is the only real genre (perhaps the drama is, too, but only to an extent) the subject of which is *time*. No other form of art can deal with that, and yet it is the driving force of the novel. And therefore I regret when the novel in the twentieth century begins to move toward poetry." (Note that this was written by a poet.)
26. Thomas Hardy, "Candour in English Fiction," quoted in J. Korg, *George Gissing: A Critical Biography,* Seattle, 1979, p. 261.

how weary we are) of puerile inventions and famishing for accuracy (I should say: reality; truth).[27]

It should now appear that I have been writing about the historicity of our knowledge, rather than about the knowledge-ability of all history; in other words, eschewing a philosophy of history but asserting the nature and evidences of a historical and monistic perspective of the world. A recognition of this, coming at the end of an age, is overdue.[28]

27. From my *Historical Consciousness* (1984 edition), p. 341. Earlier (1968 edition) I wrote "that the Western world has yet to see the appearance of a truly classic historian, a historian Dante, a historian Shakespeare." "To this I shall add, eighteen years later, that I have grown more certain of this every year: that sooner or later someone, with all the natural ease of genius, will suddenly reveal to us a new kind of history for which there will have been hardly any precedent. I am no prophet, and historian enough to despise prognostication, but here I am somehow compelled to speculate that this might occur in the twenty-first century, and perhaps even sooner than that."

28. Of course I have not been alone in this. Here are a few random samples. Owen Barfield around 1980: "The Western outlook emphasizes the importance of *history* and pays an ever increasing attention to it. . . . There is a new concept of *history* in the air, a new feeling of its true significance. We have witnessed the dim dawning of a sense that history is to be grasped as something substantial to the being of man, as an 'existential encounter.'" (Barfield wrote this around the time when slogans about "post-historic man" and "the end of history" became current.) The epigrammatic Ortega y Gasset a generation earlier: "History is not only seeing, it is thinking what has been seen. And in one sense or another, thinking is always construction." "I am a man who truly loves the past. Traditionalists, on the other hand, do not love it; they want it to be not past but present." "Man is not a *res cogitans* but a *res dramatica*. He does not exist because he thinks, but, on the contrary, he thinks because he exists." "In short, man has no nature, but instead he has . . . history." "The dawning of a new age of historical reason." The historian Johan Huizinga (1935): "Historical thinking has entered our very blood."

THREE

The Question of Scientific Knowledge

✦

"There is the belief that the expansion of the material and intellectual powers of mankind is always Progress. This has its, at first not always visible, limits. And the more the faith in Progress, including its implicit optimism, presses against these limits, the ever greater are the dangers. Perhaps one can illustrate this with a simile. With the seemingly limitless extension of its material powers mankind seems to be in the situation of a captain, whose great ship is so strongly built of steel and iron that his magnetic compass indicates the ferrous mass of the vessel, but not the position of the magnetic North. Such a ship cannot reach its goal; it will sail around in circles and eventually become a subject of the winds and the tides. . . . This danger exists so long as the captain fails to realize that his compass no longer reacts to the magnetic forces of the earth."

Werner Heisenberg, in Das Naturbild der heutigen Physik, *Hamburg, 1955.*

Evolution of my doubts. • The history of
science. • Cosmological absurdities. • The
collapse of determinism. • Darwin, Marx, Freud,
Einstein. • The ending of materialism.

I must have been very young when I learned — no, recognized — that the competence of a man, important
though it might be in particular situations, is secondary,
indeed, subordinated to the inclinations of his mind. In
the Hungary of the 1930s and the early 1940s, where I was born
and grew up, this was so among all kinds of people, including
mechanics and other workers. What mattered — surely in the
long run, but often instantly, too — was their relationship to
other people, which depended on their ideas, rather than on
their management of things. The first was more complicated —
and changeable — than the latter, and also much more consequential. And the same was true of everyone else, including
teachers, lawyers, doctors, scholars — yes, even poets and paint-
ers — and of the most reputed professors of science. There were
their achievements, and their impressive credentials; but their
credentials were one thing, and their credibility another. What
mattered were the ideas they adopted or represented or wore —

the ideas they had chosen and that they, on occasion, preferred to wear. In sum: the inclinations of their minds. After all, everything a man does depends on some kind of belief. He will speak or act in a certain way *because* he thinks that this kind of speaking or acting is better than another. I was neither intelligent nor mature enough to recognize this or state it thus; what I, and just about everybody else, thought and asked and said during those dreadful and dangerous times of World War II was simply: what kind of man is A.? That "what kind of man?" is not a simple question of category but one that is inevitably dependent on the inclinations of his mind and on the ideas he prefers to choose did not occur to me then, in the spring of my life; but it did later and it does now.

When I then became an avid reader and student of history, whether at the university or at home, I recognized the — to me, already then antiquated — nature of Objectivity: meaning principally the ideal (and, alas, so often the pretense) of an absolute and antiseptic separation of the observer from the subject or object of his observation. I had a great respect for historians who knew an impressive amount about their subject: but when their presentation, and especially their language, revealed their political, ideological, national, personal inclinations, I felt (and later saw) that the inclinations mattered very much; indeed, that the presentation of their professional competence was often subordinated to it. I did not yet understand that this was particularly so in the study of history, where the observer and the observed belong to the same species: but the "objective" word lost its unalloyed golden validity. (For a few years thereafter I was inclined to subjectivism; but I very soon recognized the futility of that, too — indeed of the entire objective/subjective antithesis: two sides of the same outdated and debased coin.)

In my life in the United States there was a certain duality between my existential and intellectual experiences. I was thankful for my escape from a Communist Hungary, and especially for the survival of many nineteenth-century institutions and customs of freedom that existed in the United States. At the same time I knew that the ideals of Scientific Objectivity in academic life (even among historians) were antiquated and flawed. They did not correspond to reality. Nor did they correspond to the characters of many of the men and women who still believed (or, perhaps, professed to believe) in them. But this went beyond the hypocrisies of academics. Among intellectuals its evidences were there in their everyday discourse; and they were there in the pronouncements of scientists. And when I learned that not only the ideal but the very nature of Objectivity had been found to be experimentally moot within the very realm of "Science," — that is, within the basic study of matter itself — this was more than a confirmation of some of my doubts.[1] It is a realization that has governed my thinking and teaching and writing of history ever since then.

Still — it is possible (and there exist, fortunately, examples of it) for a historian or a scientist or, indeed, for any thinking man to present evidences, from a proper employment of sources,

1. Wendell Berry: " . . . coming from me, who . . . have no competence or learning in science. The issue I am attempting to deal with, however, is not knowledge but ignorance. In ignorance I believe I may pronounce myself a fair expert."

that are *contrary* to his prejudices, or to his politics, or indeed to the inclinations of his mind. Whenever this happens, it manifests itself in his decision to present (which usually means: *not to exclude*) evidences *not* supporting his ideas or theses.[2] Something — not merely by the external material evidence, but something internal and spiritual — compels him to do so. I prefer not to name this kind of intellectual (and moral) probity "objective" (or even "detached").[3] "Objectivity" is a method: I prefer the word *honesty,* which is something else (and more) than a method: within it there resides at least a modicum of humility (and in history, being the knowledge that human beings have of other human beings, even a spark of understanding, of a human empathy).

It was because of the accepted equivalence of "objective" with "scientific" that my early skepticism about Objectivism in history included an element of doubt whether to consider History as a Science. It took me some time to recognize that history was not — or, more precisely, was *no longer*[4] — a Science. It took

2. Including overcoming the habit of excluding bibliographical or referential credits or mentions of works of people one dislikes.
3. Luke 17:20–21: "And being asked by the Pharisees, when the kingdom of God should come? he answered them, and said: the kingdom of God cometh not with observation. Neither shall they say: Behold here, or behold there. For lo, the kingdom of God is within you."
4. *No longer:* because the notion, or idea, of History as a Science was, by and large, typical of the nineteenth century. (During the eighteenth century history was seen as an important branch of literature.) In the twen-

me a little longer to recognize something more important, which is the subordination of science to history—the former being inevitably part of the latter, and not the reverse.

But then this is very simple. In the order of time—whether according to Genesis or to Evolution—first came Nature; then came Man; and then the Science of Nature. Like everything else, Science has its history because of the men and women who have thought of it and worked at it. No scientists, no Science. This is so obvious that it needs no explanation. But before we recognize some of its consequences we must look, for a moment, at the evolution of the meaning of "Scientist."

"Scientist" is—certainly in English—more recent than we are accustomed to think. The *Oxford English Dictionary* marks its first appearance in 1840. That year the biologist William Whewell, who was a forerunner of Darwin, wrote: "We need very much a name to describe a cultivator of science in general. I should incline to call him a Scientist." In the same year an article in *Blackwood's Edinburgh Magazine* distinguished "scientist" from "artist." But soon a distinction between scientist and other scholars took root: "scientist" was a term applicable to practitioners of "natural" (that is, physical) sciences. And this is how the sense and the meaning not only of "scientist" but also of "science" has narrowed ever since. When we think of a Scientist we think of a man or woman in a laboratory, perhaps in a white coat. The widespread sense of this is such that even after the

---

tieth century many historians tried to qualify the nineteenth-century concept thus: History was (is) a Social Science. It is not: it is a form of thought.

appearance and acceptance of the social sciences (for example, of sociology or psychology), people apply the noun "scientist" to sociologists or psychologists rarely, if at all. This is not so in some other languages — in German, for example, where the words "Wissenschaft" and "Wissenschaftler": "knowledge" and "scholar" still include practitioners of the physical and of the human "sciences" alike. But there, too, "Wissenschaftler" is applied to a practitioner of the humanities less and less often. In sum: the application of the word "scientist" to an accredited professional practitioner of the natural sciences has, during the twentieth century, become nearly universal.[5]

Yet throughout most of history, and throughout most of the Modern Age, the meaning of the venerable words "scholar" and "scholarship" included astronomers as well as historians, chemists as well as philosophers, mathematicians as well as philologists. Indeed, something very typical of the Modern Age was the — perhaps typically bourgeois — respect and support for artists or scholars offered by their patrons. It is pleasant — more: it is charming — to read that in the sixteenth century a *curieux* in French meant an "intellectual." (Four hundred years later, at the end of the twentieth century, "intellectual" — especially the noun — designating certain people has lost much of its once approbatory shine.) During at least four centuries of the Modern Age, "scholar" meant a serious and modest and withdrawn man, whose interest and devotion to his, often unusual, subjects

5. The Germans were aware of this: hence the insistence of their philosopher Wilhelm Dilthey, about 125 years ago, to distinguish between "Natur" and "Geisteswissenschaften": between natural/physical and spiritual/mental "sciences."

was inseparable from the openness of his mind *(curieux)* and from the qualities of his character: a man of probity. This kind of respect has largely waned now, except perhaps here and there. There are too many so-called scientists, and there are all kinds among them — this is how many people are now inclined to see them. As in almost every other field of life, inflation has set in: when there is more and more of something it is worth less and less.

However — the trouble lies elsewhere. We cannot restore the old-fashioned meaning of "scholar," for more than one reason. We must accept the present sense and definition of a Scientist — a person of certified knowledge and competence, distinct and different from the holders of other kinds of advanced degrees, since both the objects and the purposes of his studies and of his business are different. Objects, yes: a man who is a cancer researcher is working at an application of natural science that has at least the potential of a beneficial effect on human lives. But purpose: that is a more complicated matter. There are all kinds of microbiologists as there are all kinds of sociologists, good and bad people among them; and the quality of their purposes is a question of their characters, which may have little or nothing to do with the object of their researches, or even with the recognition of their competence among their professional colleagues. They are — as are all of us — fallible human beings.

Whether one believes or does not believe that human fallibility has been ordained by God, there can be no argument that human fallibility is inevitably connected with the complexity of human nature — because of the functions of the human mind.

And this is where, despite the many extraordinary and impressive applications of science, the trouble with the present (and during the past 150 years narrowing) concepts of Science and Scientists enter.

The human being is not the largest or the strongest or the longest living organism in the universe. But his organism is the most complex one in it. (That is *one* of the reasons to consider the uniqueness of human beings and of the earth within the entire universe.) In every one of their fields scientists are dealing with organisms that are less complex than is the human one. There are, of course, innumerable examples where the applied results of experiments with animal or mineral or vegetable substances have benefited and will continue to benefit mankind. There is now, alas, a growing number of such experiments whose results are questionable: genetic "engineering," for example. They are questionable — to say the least — because of the potential harm of their effects on human life and nature on this earth. But this is not what I am now writing about. My interest, and concern, is with the belief according to which the treatment and the results of the knowledge of more primitive organisms are taken as naturally and automatically applicable (if not altogether superior) to our knowledge of the most complex of organisms in the universe. My argument is not only that the knowledge — and treatment — of human beings by other human beings is more important than their knowledge of less complex organisms. It is that when we come to the history of Science — that is, of scientists — this also involves the relationships of some of the most complex organisms in the universe: in sum, with the relationships of scientists among themselves, with scientists as human beings.

The notion that the subjects of Science are "reality" itself, outside of us, to be discovered by present and future scientists, driving out every working morning with their ever more advanced instruments, returning every night after having hacked at the Mountain Range of Science, bringing back tiny or large but in any case promising bits of it, is, alas, still widespread — but it is also silly. No use to berate it further, except perhaps to note that by the end of the twentieth century this notion may be less widespread than one hundred and more years ago: a slow recognition, proceeding apace with the occasional recognition of the fallibility of Science — that is, of Scientists. But during the twentieth century an enormously significant contribution to such a recognition has been admitted — sometimes willingly, often unwillingly; sometimes openly, often obscurely and implicitly — by scientists themselves.

This has happened in the history of physics — which is more than just one branch of science, physics being the basic study of matter. There was a great revolution in physics during the first quarter of the century; there was a revolution, too, in applied physics that culminated in 1945 with the explosion of the first atomic bomb. (After that: Sound and Fury, Signifying Little.)[6] In 1900 the German physicist Max Planck dis-

---

6. See below, pp. 102 ff. It may be said that since 1927, because of the affirmation of the Uncertainty or Indeterminacy principle, physics is no longer separable from metaphysics — just as philosophy is no longer separable from epistemology. The latter, often regarded as a branch of philoso-

covered that in certain situations energy does not proceed regularly but in jumps: these jumps he called quanta.[7] Around the same time scientists discovered a new element—radium—the very substance of which was changing in time. In 1905 came Einstein's relativity theory, again introducing time (whose existence is one thing, but whose measurability is nothing but a human endeavor) into the relationships of energy and mass. Twenty years later the young German physicist Werner Heisenberg not only discovered but proved that in certain subatomic situations neither classical objectivity nor mechanical causality applied: that the act of the physicist's observation (more exactly: his attempts at measurement) interfered either with the movement or with the situation of his object—which meant, among other things, a big crack in the fundament of Descartes's and Newton's objectivism and determinism. In other words: the study of the "reality" of matter was inseparable from the

---

phy, means the study of the philosophy of knowledge: but there are reasons to argue that all philosophy must be regarded as epistemology now. One can no more separate the philosopher from his philosophy than one can separate the physicist from his physics. In both cases the important question is no longer *what* he knows but *how* he knows it. (And *why:* the "why" being ever so often implicit in the "how.")

7. A primitive illustration: turn down the spigot until the flow of water is reduced to single drops. Talking of quantified energy is as little and as much meaningful as talking of "dropified" water. (This formulation in a letter from the Norwegian physicist Torger Holtsmark.) Also: In 1900 Planck's choice of the word "quantum" may have had something to do with the intellectual currency of the word in Germany at that time. Nietzsche, who died in the same moment (August 1900) when Planck made his discovery, had written earlier, in *The Will to Power,* about "quanta of power that determine and distinguish rank."

interference (and from the mind and the purpose) of the scientist.

What happened in the 1920s and after was of course inseparable from the history of physicists — indeed, from the history of their times. The 1920s, sometimes called the Golden Age of Physics, was, too, part of a greater development, a phase in the political, cultural, ideological, intellectual history of Europe. This was the primacy of Germany — and of German science and German thinking — in the history of the world, or at least of Europe, approximately from 1870 to 1941. Much of this primacy survived Germany's defeat after World War I: of this the rise of Berlin as the cultural capital of Europe in the 1920s and the German leadership in the advancement of physics were but two examples.

There was more to this too, on another, deeper level. What Germany represented was a reaction to (or, rather, a move away from) the French cult of Reason, to the Age of Enlightenment, with its concordant materialism. Germany was the land of neo-idealism, a national tendency which soon debouched into an idealistic determinism of which Adolf Hitler was the principal and, for a while, the most diabolically successful representative. And — lest my readers think that these are but the cerebrations of a philosophical historian — in the 1920s there were plenty of evidences of the struggles between differing mental inclinations among German physicists themselves. Certain ones among them (Philipp Lenard and Johannes Stark, both Nobel Prize winners) attacked and dismissed Einstein's relativity theory because Einstein was a Jew and a "pacifist," meaning: non-German and anti-German. Then, even after Heisenberg's indeterminacy principle had been proved and accepted by the majority of the leading physicists, Einstein refused to accept it. He remained a convinced determinist during the rest of his life, fiddling uselessly with unsuccessful experiments and formulations hoping to disprove indeterminacy in Princeton, with no effect to his enduring reputation.[8]

There is plenty of recorded evidence, usually buried in recondite journals addressed to the history of science, about these controversies among physicists in the 1920s — between people who believed or disbelieved this or that, because they wished to believe this and disbelieve that. One of the finer minds among this stellar generation of physicists, the Austrian Erwin Schrödinger (another Nobel Prize winner, though one whose career declined into an unfulfilling cul-de-sac) as early as 1932 said in a lecture at the Prussian Academy of Sciences that, yes, Science can be (and often is) A Fashion of the Times, a consequence of The Temper of the Age (his formulation). Even earlier, in

---

8. "In the 1920s the indeterminacy revolution in physics coincided with the defeat of the 'Left' in Europe. . . . In 1930, at the Brussels-Solvay Congress of International Physics, Einstein, refusing to admit the Heisenberg Uncertainty principle, suffered a humiliating defeat, which was then administered by Bohr. I am not saying that this was a political event. I am saying that this event, and the time of its occurrence, has a significance in the general cultural history of Europe, including its politics to some extent. For there is a certain correspondence between Einstein's defeat in 1930 and the failure of German Marxism with its interpretation of Economic Man, at that very historical moment. They were, both, failures of the deterministic thinking of the nineteenth century; and in view of more universal historical developments of that time, it is at least significant that this happened in 1930." Lukacs, *The Last European War, 1939–1941,* New York, 1976, p. 524, note 194.

1913, the great French physicist (and historian of science) Pierre Duhem wrote: "The study of the method of physics is powerless to disclose to the physicist the reason leading him to construct a physical theory."[9] And the physicists' dependence on accepted and acceptable ideas within the general climates of opinion, and of course especially on those within their profession, was demonstrated, often tellingly, by physicists and historians of physics — among them Karl v. Meyenn, Paul Forman, Gerald Holton, John L. Heilbronner, Ludwig Fleck,[10] and others during the twentieth century — many of them well before the eventually celebrated tergiversations of Thomas Kuhn. And toward the end of the century the French physicist Bernard D'Espagnat: "Physicists are like all other men. When, by and large, an allegory seems to be running well, their tendency is, bit by

9. "Is Science a Fashion of the Times?" An English version of Schrödinger's lecture, in Chapter IV of *Science and the Human Temperament,* New York, 1935. Duhem, *Notice sur les titres et travaux scientifiques,* Bordeaux, 1913, pp. 227–228. About Duhem see Chapter 5, pp. 195–202.

10. Karl von Meyenn, *Quantenmechanik und Weimarer Republik,* Braunschweig, 1994, p. 9: "When it comes to the emergence of a new idea in science, the first task would be to clarify the part played in it by the influence of the cultural atmosphere ["Kulturmilieu"] and the part played by the influence of the psychic make-up of the individual researcher." Ludwig Fleck, *Genesis and Development of a Scientific Fact,* Chicago, 1979 (original edition in German, Basel, 1935): "Facts are the results of styles of thought." Fleck traced at least one particular instance of how the results of a laboratory discovery led to a different, and then widely accepted, result in medical biology (the so-called Wassermann reaction). P. 21: "It is nonsense to think that the history of cognition has as little to do with science as, for example, the history of the telephone with telephone conversations. At least three-quarters, if not the entire context of science is conditioned by the history of ideas, psychology, the sociology of ideas, and is thus explicable in these terms."

bit, to hypostatize the concept and never question it among themselves — and before their students — as if that concept were, really, the ultimate *thing*.[11] In *The Two Cultures*, C. P. Snow wrote that Science has "an automatic corrective." It does not.[12]

Haunted by suspicions and anxieties, by the 1930s, the world of the physicists and the minds of many of them were split, but just as the atomic nucleus would be — in 1938 in Berlin. We must (I wrote more than a quarter-century ago), for the sake of reality, insist on the human element in these events:

> The history of science is the history of scientists,
> just as the history of the universe is the history of
> man. It is history, . . . that explains both how and
> why the atomic bomb was made. The "causes" of
> the atom bomb are historical and, ultimately,
> personal; they are scientific and technical only on

11. Bernard D'Espagnat, *Regards sur la matière des quanta et des choses* (with Etienne Klein), Paris, 1993, pp. 279–280. D'Espagnat continues: "High-energy physicists, depending on their utilization of *Feynman's Diagrams* (which symbolize calculations of future observations) fall into the same error, which consists of regarding those diagrams as if they were true images of existing objects. This presents no danger for the practices of their research . . . but it is a mental impoverishment that may, in the long run, lead to an inadequate, exaggerated, or underestimated appreciation of the purpose of research." C. S. Lewis, *The Pilgrim's Regress:* "Hypothesis, my dear young friend, establishes itself by a cumulative process; or, to use popular language, if you make the same guess often enough it ceases to be a guess and becomes a scientific fact."
12. An eventually belated corrective, perhaps — but only in the sense in which George Orwell wrote that the difference between a good and a bad poem is that the latter does not survive.

a secondary (mechanical) level of "causes." The principal causes of the making of the bomb include the Second World War, Hitler, and the persecution of Jews by the Germans. The bomb was made when it was made, not merely because at a certain phase in the development of science a certain stage of technological know-how was reached, but principally because at a certain time in history in the minds of certain eminent refugee scientists, the fear had arisen that German scientists might be building an atomic bomb for Hitler. Technically speaking, the important stages in the history of the atomic bomb were the splitting of the uranium nucleus by neutrons in December 1938, the functioning of the first nuclear reactor in Chicago in December 1942, the exploding of the first bomb in New Mexico in July 1945, and the two bombs finally cast on Japan in August 1945; but the technological character of these stages must not obscure the principal factors in their achievement which, as in every historical event, were the results of personal choices, and conditioned by the political, national, religious, intellectual and ideological inclinations of the minds of responsible men.[13]

13. *The Last European War, 1939–1941*, New York, 1976 (new ed., New Haven, 2001, pp. 523–524).

In 1945, immediately after the German surrender, a group of the most eminent German physicists was whisked to England, where they were interned, in civil and comfortable conditions, in a house named Farm Hall. Their British hosts were interested to learn what these men knew. The walls contained secret microphones; their conversations were recorded; and then published forty-seven years later. When, on the morrow of the Hiroshima bomb, the internees were first informed of what had just happened, their reactions were of course interesting; but when we read that transcript of their agitated debates, their scientific and technical arguments (many of which were wrong) are less interesting today than were their political and moral arguments among themselves.

I wrote earlier about the history of physics after 1945: Sound and Fury, Signifying Little. These are harsh words. What I mean is that after 1945 the general intellectual crisis at the end of the Modern Age reached the realm of physics: perhaps the only realm that had made a great contribution in the 1920s to the intellectual history of the world. In 1955 Einstein died. The same year Heisenberg delivered his Gifford Lectures in which he explained the philosophical essence and the epistemological consequences of Indeterminacy. Working on the first draft of my book *Historical Consciousness,* I tried to find physicists whom I could ask what they thought of the meaning of Heisenberg's epistemological propositions. I got nowhere: those were things about which they were unwilling to think — and to speak.[14] Around that time I noticed how, here and there,

14. Eventually I wrote Heisenberg and visited him, but only for the simple

the unquestioning belief in timeless scientific certitudes was cracking. There appeared in 1962 Thomas S. Kuhn's *The Structure of Scientific Revolutions* — interestingly, around the same time as Carr's earlier cited *What Is History?* (1961), advancing from Objectivism to Subjectivism ("before you study the history, study the historian"). Kuhn wrote that Science is, after all, the result of "a consensus of the scientific community" — in plainer English, the result of scientists. I thought that Wilde's aphorism about certain thinkers applied to these intellectuals perfectly: they were pursuing the obvious with the enthusiasm of shortsighted detectives. At least Carr's book was fairly well written (though poorly thought out), while Kuhn's still sometimes celebrated work amounted to the errant cerebration of a flat-footed academic, often substituting vocabulary for thought.[15]

---

purpose of assuring myself that I had understood his propositions properly enough.

15. A few examples, from successive pages of Kuhn's book. P. viii: [I was] "led to recognize in scientific research of what I have since called 'paradigms.' These I take to be universally recognized scientific achievements that for a time provide model problems and solutions to a community of practitioners." (This is *not* what "paradigm" means.) P. 7: A new paradigm is "seldom completed by a single man and never overnight. No wonder historians have had difficulty to dating precisely this extended process that their vocabulary impels them to view as an isolated event." ("Their vocabulary?" Does it?) P. 8. "History, we too often say, is a purely descriptive discipline." (Is it "purely descriptive"? And is "description" a "discipline"?) P. 80: "Science has seemed to provide so apt an illustration of the generalization that truth and falsity are uniquely and unequivocally determined by the confrontation of statement with fact." (Do facts mean anything apart from their statements?) P. 103: "Successive paradigms tell us different things about the population of the universe and about that population's behavior." (Do they?) Enough of this.

(One of the lamentable consequences of his text arose from his frequent employment of the unattractive word "paradigm" — "the status of community paradigms," etc., etc. — an unattractive word that thereafter became fashionable in intellectual commerce.)

But something more significant and worrisome than the symptomatic appearance of such books was happening in physics itself. While discovering (in essence constructing, or rather, naming) more and more minuscule atomic particles, physics was now moving into a sphere of abstractions, seeking for a Unified Theory of the Universe, to the senselessness of which I shall return. Heisenberg himself was not unaffected by this. During the last twenty years of his life (he died in 1976) he was struggling with the possibility of a mathematical model, an equation that would perhaps, and permanently, formulate our knowledge of the fundamentals of physics. Meanwhile the meaning of his great early contribution, that of the inescapable involvement of the physicist with the physics of matter was, if not altogether ignored, brushed aside by another generation of ambitious young physicists, including Nobel laureates such as Richard Feynman and Murray Gell-Mann and Steven Weinberg.

It is true that Heisenberg's discoveries involve only extreme and subatomic situations. Meanwhile, in the mechanical world, including all of its wonders such as space rockets or the Internet, the essential "laws" and causalities of Newtonian physics continue to apply. But there are more and more evidences in the human world, where more and more of us recognize how observation may affect — indeed, it often does affect — the nature of the object, perhaps especially in the age of democracy. That "polls" — of all kinds — may not only influence but actually create the very conditions of elections, that is, of choices; that advertisements of popularity can lead to popularity (repeating and repeating that someone or something is popular may make him, or it, popular): these are but two of the many examples of such a recognition. Another is the increasing use of such terms as "perception" or "image"; another recognition that such *are* components of reality itself. When it comes to the study of our most intellectual organ, the human eye, there are more and more evidences that perception is not the packaging or the categorizing of sensation, but that it is an inescapable component of sensation itself, and indeed, *simultaneous* with it[16] — as are imagination and memory — inseparable from, and not merely consequent to, the act of seeing.

Throughout the Modern Age (indeed, until the "revolution" in physics during the first quarter of the twentieth century) it was taken for granted that our laws of physics were the same everywhere and at any time — including the whole universe, and the many millions of years before man appeared on earth. I do not think that we needed the proof of uncertainty/ indeterminacy to see that such a belief is both naive and arrogant, but perhaps this is not my main argument here. The

16. And, in some instances, perception may indeed *precede* sensation. See below, pp. 131, 137.

point is that by the end of the twentieth century the quest of physicists for a unified theory of the universe had become an — at times laughable — absurdity, because of the very character of their theorizing, and because of its categorical application to theories of the universe. About the first I cannot improve on the statements by David Lindley, a theoretical physicist — and astronomer — himself (also a senior editor of *Science*). Because of their increasing tendency to make everything dependent on abstruse mathematical formulations,

> the most recent speculation of the theoretical physicists is that elementary particles are not particles at all but vibrations of tiny loops of quantum-mechanical string, wriggling around in twenty-six-dimensional space. This is the modern equivalent of the classical physicist's hope that all matter could be understood in terms of atoms that behaved essentially like little billiard balls. . . . Modern particle physics is, in a literal sense, incomprehensible. It is grounded not in the tangible and testable notions of objects and points and pushes and pulls but in a sophisticated and indirect mathematical language of fields and interactions and wave-functions. The old concepts are in there somewhere, but in heavy disguise. To the outsider, it may seem that the theoretical physicists of today are in the grip of a collective mathematical zaniness, inventing twenty-six-dimensional spaces and filling them

with strings out of obfuscatory glee. Their use of language is as esoteric and baffling as that of the literary deconstructionists: they seem to speak in words and sentences, but it is a kind of code. . . . Each speaks in a private gobbledygook understandable only to those similarly initiated.

In one sense, such criticism of modern theoretical physics is philistine . . . [but] the inexorable progress of physics from the world we can see and touch into a world made accessible only by huge and expensive experimental equipment, and on into a world illuminated by the intellect alone, is a genuine cause for alarm. [When] the trend toward increasing abstraction is turning theoretical physics into recreational mathematics, endlessly amusing to those who can master the technique and join the game, [it becomes] ultimately meaningless because the objects of mathematical manipulation are forever beyond the access of experiment and measurement. . . . [Is that] another milestone on the road to the end of physics? . . . What is the use of a theory that looks attractive but contains no additional power of prediction, and makes no statement that can be tested? Does physics then become a branch of aesthetics?[17]

17. David Lindley, *The End of Physics: The Myth of a Unified Theory,* New York, 1993, pp. 18–20.

A (The?) Theory of Everything cannot be but an illusion; and even a profitable illusion amounts to less than a myth.[18] What, then, are both illusory and arrogant are the cerebrations of physicists and astronomers about the universe (Big Bang, Black Holes, and so on) in our very times, facilitated by more and more expensive instruments, radiotelescopes, supercolliders. This confluence of theoretical physics and cosmology was, of course, predictable, since physics both pretends and claims universality (whence its assumption to ascertain how the universe came about and how it evolves) whereby present cosmology depends on a unified theory, on a finally completed understanding of the "laws" of physics. But the very fundament of this alleged dependence is false. The known and visible and measurable conditions of the universe are not *anterior* but *consequent* to our existence and to our consciousness.[19] The universe is such as it is because in the center of it there exist conscious and participant people who can see it, explore it, study it. Such an insistence on the centrality, and on the uniqueness, of human beings is a statement not of arrogance but of its very contrary, perhaps

18. Goethe to Eckermann (1827) about professors who are unwilling to change their minds even in face of contradictory evidence. " 'This is not to be wondered at,' said Goethe: 'such people continue in error because they are indebted to it for their existence. They would otherwise have to learn everything over again, and that would be very inconvenient.' 'But,' said I, 'how can their experiments prove the truth when the basis of their doctrine is false?' 'They do *not* prove the truth,' said Goethe, 'nor is such the intention; the only point with these professors is to prove their own opinion.' " (Rathenau, *circa* 1921: "There are no specialists; there are only vested interests.")
19. To this I may add — for God-believers — that the world has been created by God for the existence and the consciousness of human beings.

even of humility: a recognition of the inevitable limitations of mankind.

Here is an example of cosmological nonsense by a physicist, Steven Weinberg: "The universe is very large, and it should be no surprise that, among the enormous number of planets that support only unintelligent life and the still vaster number of planets that cannot support life at all, there is some tiny fraction on which there are living beings who are capable of thinking about the universe, as we are doing here."[20] Whereupon I wrote: "What kind of language — and logic — is this? *'No surprise'*? Consider: 'The five boroughs of New York City are very large, *and it should be no surprise* that, among the enormous number of its inhabitants who do not walk and the still vaster number who do not like to walk at all, there is some tiny fraction who are able to levitate.'"[21]

The propagation of such cosmological absurdities is of course also facilitated by the manufacture of more and more "powerful" — and more and more expensive — telescopes, the use of which and the photographs through which, however, are ultimately dependent on the limitations of the human eye — that is, on the very act of seeing. On the other microscopic end of the spectrum the present situation is even more absurd. Consider that during the last decades physicists have "found" more and more subatomic particles. I put "found" within quotation marks, since it is they who — with the help of bigger and bigger and more and more expensive atom-smashers, have produced

20. *American Scholar,* Summer 1999.
21. Ibid., Autumn 1999.

these very particles themselves. These atom-smashers — nowadays named supercolliders — accelerate atomic particles at fantastic speeds, smashing atoms into smaller and smaller bits. The supercolliders require enormous amounts of space for their tunnels and they are enormously expensive. (The funding of $8.4 billion for the largest one of them in Texas was abandoned in 1993.) Their proponents tend to argue that with their help Science may discover the smallest building block of the universe, or thus arrive at the Grand Unified Theory of Physics. But of course their main problem concerns something more fundamental than cost.

The reduction of the universe to an essential basic particle was first attempted by Democritus in the fifth century B.C. — theoretically, since he had no microscopes or atom-smashers at his disposal. Democritus gave us the name and the theory of the atom, establishing it as the basic unit of matter, a notion that has not changed for more than two thousand years. He was a materialist: he believed that the human soul itself (including the air we breathe) consists of nothing but atoms. He also believed and stated that the atom was absolutely indivisible. We now know that this is not so: during the twentieth century physicists have found — or, more precisely, produced — other, smaller particles. But what is the nature of some of these particles? They — more exactly: their tracks and patterns — are produced by the scientists themselves. And when it comes to subatomic particles we cannot speak of their "essence" or their "matter" but only of situations — events and not "facts"[22] — that occur during and

22. About this, see below, pp. 133–135.

because of our measurements of matter. Heisenberg proved this more than seventy years ago: it is not possible to exclude the observer from what he measures.

Now consider the names physicists have given to many of these particles — names that are often nothing but tortuous linguistic inventions. The above-cited Lindley wrote that "the quality of nomenclature in particle physics [has sunk] to new lows." Well after physicists discovered the "neutrino" (to be distinguished from the "neutron") we now have "selectrons" and "sneutrinos" and "worst of all, the whole set of quarks turns into a corresponding set of 'squarks.' Where the addition of an initial S doesn't work, diminutive endings have been resorted to, producing a 'photino' to go with the photon, 'gluinos' for gluons." Thus, after more than five hundred years, we are back in the presence of medieval superstition of nominalism: the tendency to believe that once we give a name to a phenomenon we've "got it." That is the very opposite of realism, which in philosophy, art — indeed, in all intellectual endeavors — began to replace nominalism around the time of the Renaissance, at the very beginning of the Modern Age.

Near the end of the Middle Ages, a few theologians (the "scientists" of that time) persuaded a king of France to give them permission for an experiment that had been forbidden by the Church. They were allowed to weigh the soul of a criminal by measuring him both before and after his hanging. As usually happens with academics, they came up with a definite result: the soul weighed about an ounce and a half. We laugh at such things, of course. But remember how much suffering, how such ideas about the soul were current in the religious struggles during the transition from the Middle Ages to the Modern Age. (Not to speak of the fact that the soul-weighing experiment was somewhat less costly than the supercollider.) We ought at least consider the possibility that a few centuries hence people may laugh at the pretensions of some of our scientists, as well as at our gullibility at the end of the twentieth century and at the beginning of the twenty-first.

We have seen that the earlier assumption — that the physical essence of the entire universe would be revealed in our discovery of its original and smaller particle — has now degenerated into the second assumption, the myth of the Unified Theory: that many physicists are now inclined to believe that even if we cannot find the smallest building block of the universe, we can find a mathematical formula that will explain the entire universe: a Theory of Everything. Indeed it is more and more likely that supercolliders may *not* "produce" the basic unit of the universe, while they may create more subatomic situations that might be formulated mathematically. But: most mathematical formulas about atomic matters remain untested and untestable, since they are theoretical and abstract. The belief that the universe is written in the language of mathematics is entirely outdated.[23] "What is there exact in mathematics except its own exactitude?" Goethe wrote. He was right, as many mathematicians themselves in the twentieth century have confirmed.[24]

---

23. George Santayana, *My Host the World,* 122: "It is a marvel that mathematics should apply so well to the material world, [but] to apply it to history or ideas is pure madness."
24. The mathematician Kurt Gödel's 1931 theorem — a kind of odd *pendant* to Heisenberg's 1925 Uncertainty.

My argument is not simply that it is not given to human beings to explain or know everything, including the universe. When human beings recognize that they cannot create everything and cannot see everything and cannot define everything, such limitations do not impoverish but enrich the human mind. (Another example of how the "laws" of physics do not apply to many of the functions of the human mind.) We must recognize, too, that our concepts of matter, and of the universe, are *models*. A model is man-made, dependent on its inventor. More important: the model cannot, and must not, be mistaken for the world.

Without the recognition of these limitations "Science" and the still current meaning of "Progress" would, as George Gissing wrote at the dawn of the twentieth century, "restore barbarism under a mark of civilization; I see it darkening men's minds and hardening their hearts." Or, as Johan Huizinga wrote in his debate with the French rationalist Julien Benda in 1933: "Our common enemy is the fearful master, the spirit of technology. We must not underestimate its power."

The fundament (and the unavoidable component) of determinism, and of Objectivism, and of what Descartes established as "the scientific method," is mechanical causality. Mechanical causality means three things. First: that the same causes must — always and everywhere — have the same effects. Second, that there must be an equivalence between the force of cause and that of its effect. Third: that the cause must always and everywhere precede its effect.

Neither wisdom nor profound philosophic disquisitions are needed to point out that this kind of causality does *not* always — indeed, *not* really — apply to human life (again: to the lives of the most complex organisms in the entire universe). The principal element, or instrument, that disrupts these causalities is the human mind. It intrudes into the structure (and also into the sequence) of events: because what happens is inseparable from what one thinks (or from what most people think) happens. This is true about such sensual experiences as pain or pleasure as much as it is about money or wars, about prices on the stock exchange or about the clashes of vast armies. (We may — later — realize that what we had thought happened was wrong: but such an eventual recognition does not negate the existence, and the consequences, of our earlier recognition. The later, chastened, recognition occurs not because of our "scientific" but because of our historical consciousness, including the variable functions of our memory.)

A mechanical cause-effect relationship or equivalence *may* apply to the human body, but only to the physical body in its mindless (or lifeless) state. We can predict at what pressure a bone will break, or what amount of a chemical injection will stop the function of a certain organ: the precise margin, or extent, of intolerability. But this excludes the human mind. "Intolerable" is, simply (or, rather, complicatedly?) what a man thinks is intolerable, what he no longer wishes to tolerate. This is as true of single persons as it is of large numbers of people. There are people brave under torture and people weak under torture, and their relative and momentarily extant bravery or weakness has nothing to do with the calcium content of the bone of their thumb pressed by the thumb-screw: one will cry out, another won't; one will confess, another will stare at his torturers. When a general reports (or rather, convinces himself) that the pressure on his lines is "intolerable," he is ready to retreat. People who ought to know better are often unable — or, rather, unwilling — to recognize this, captive as their brains are within categories of mechanical causality. In his introduction to *The History of the Second World War* (1970) the reputable British military historian Liddell Hart wrote: "If you allow anyone to stoke up a boiler until the steam-pressure rises beyond danger-point, the real responsibility for any resultant explosion will lie with you. That truth of physical science applies equally to political science — especially to the conduct of international affairs." "That truth of physical science" is no truth when it comes to human (let alone "international") affairs. It is certainly inapplicable to it. There are umpteen examples of revolutions breaking out not when the pressure, when the oppression of people, was strongest but when it had already begun to lessen — and when people sensed and recognized that. This was as true of 1789 as it was of 1917 or of 1956, of the French or the Russian or the Hungarian revolutions — as it is true of boys chafing under the martinet rule of a teacher (after, not before, the harsh discipline of the latter has begun to relax). The decisive event is not the pressure itself but the lodging of that idea in the mind. And the mind is *not* a passive instrument, even though it can and will be strongly influenced by what others think. (Again: what happens is not apart from what people think happens, because every human thought and every human act is something more than and something different from a reaction.)

With this recognition there goes the entire structure of mechanical causality. In Liddell Hart's boiler the lid will fly off at a predictable and measurable point and time, when a definite degree of pressure occurs. But human explosions do not necessarily occur at the highest point of pressure; nor are they exactly measurable and predictable. This is so not because of some kind of surviving irrationality at the core of the human species. To the contrary: in the human world the lid is not simply a passive element — the lid is thinking about itself. And this brings us to the other limitation of mechanical causality: the, seemingly commonsense, condition that a cause must necessarily precede its effect. But that is not as simple as that — again because of the intrusion of mind. Yes, we are pushed by the past; yes, many of our actions, and even thoughts, are largely reactions — but only largely; not entirely. We are also pulled by the future — more appositely: by our own sense or vision of our future.[25] Again it does not require great discernment to recognize that the pull of the future is evident in a myriad of human situations: in anticipation of pleasure or of pain as well as in the effect of anticipation on the very functioning of our bodies and senses (as when a girl who is afraid of blushing reddens, or when a man fearing inadequacy becomes impotent). In other words: there are human situations in which it may be argued that what may happen tomorrow is the "cause" of what happens today (or of what happened yesterday). Human perception often not only occurs simultaneously with sensation but actually precedes it (after all, the very act of seeing "consists," as Ortega y

25. About the difference between motives and purposes, see pp. 59–60.

Gasset put it, "of applying a previous image which we have to a present sensation").

All of the foregoing does not mean that I am merely arguing the case of Humanism against Scientism, falling back on the old and venerable and sometimes even charming romantic dualism: this is Humanism, this is Science; both have their uses, but the twain shall never meet. It would not be worth my while to write yet another, romantic and reactionary, essay or book about that. But what is important — and certainly significant — is that the shortcomings of determinism have been recognized by physicists themselves. Unfortunately, it is also significant that most of them have refused to think about the meaning of this (leaving aside the now outdated condition of people, including scientists, who had refused to acknowledge it at all).[26] Still, the meaning of the collapse of determinism has been expressed by many important physicists besides Heisenberg. Schrödinger in his 1932 Berlin lecture (even as he did not entirely distance himself from determinism) wrote that until relatively recently "it was simply a matter of taste or philosophic prejudice whether the preference was given to determinism or indeterminism. The

26. Nearly two centuries after Goethe (see above, p. 108, note 18) allow me to rephrase, less concisely, how the reasons for such an unwillingness are complicated. They include (a) an unwillingness to become preoccupied by anything outside of an ever narrowing specialization of research; (b) a nagging anxiety that an eventually widening recognition of a less than absolute (and practical) meaning of their science may affect their professional reputation; (c) that a recognition of the meaning of indeterminism would consequently impel them to rethink the validity of rationalism, of the Enlightenment, of their view of God's and man's function within the universe — from which they instinctively, and consequently intellectually, recoil.

former was favored by ancient custom, possibly by an *a priori* belief. In favor of the latter it could be argued that this ancient habit demonstrably rested on the actual laws which we observe functioning in our surroundings. As soon, however, as the great majority or possibly all of these laws are seen to be of a statistical nature, they cease to provide a rational argument for the retention of determinism."

Georges Bernanos (1946): "Between those who think that civilization is a victory of man in the struggle against the determinism of things and those who want to make of man a thing among things, there is no possible scheme of reconciliation." Wendell Berry (1999): "It is easy for me to imagine that the next great division of the world will be between people who wish to live as creatures and people who wish to live as machines."

All of the sound and fury, all of the frantic assertions of "modernity" notwithstanding, the twentieth century was largely one of intellectual (and artistic) stagnation. One evidence of this has been the protracted reputation of "modern" masters of thought, such as Darwin and Marx and Freud and Einstein, all four regarding themselves as scientists. They were regarded as modern masters at the beginning of the historic twentieth century, in 1914, as well as at its end, in 1989 — and, except perhaps for Marx, even now. Consider the amazing endurance of their prestige, most of them having lived and flourished long ago: Darwin (1812–1882), Marx (1818–1883), Freud (1856–1939), Einstein (1878–1955). Nothing like such a protracted prestige existed in previous centuries. Were we to consider who were thought the giants of intellect and of art, say, in 1820 and then in 1890, we would get an entirely different list of great names: say, Goethe, Chateaubriand, Beethoven around 1820 and Nietzsche, Ibsen, Wagner sixty or seventy years later. There *are* signs recently that the reputations of Darwin, Marx, Freud, Einstein are experiencing scattered reevaluations. This is especially so in the case of Marx, less so in the case of Freud, only occasionally in the case of Darwin, and almost not at all in the case of Einstein. But now I am compelled to sum up, no matter how briefly, my own criticism about the structure and the essence of their ideas—for the purposes of this book, which is, after all, no more than a long essay.

Darwin's reputation is still high and unblemished. He is buried in Westminster Abbey (Marx and Freud are buried elsewhere in London and Einstein in Princeton). Yet Darwin's achievement, more than that of the other three, was predictable. Other scientists—anthropologists, biologists, zoologists—were his close forerunners. The recognition that monkeys resembled men more than, say, minnows was, of course, no intellectual feat: but Darwin's achievement was the explanation of the origin of species according to a scientific system. Yet that too was inseparable from the intellectual climate of his times: from an expectable reaction to the increasingly evident inadequacy—especially in a Bible-reading and Protestant nation such as Britain—of a strictly scriptural interpretation of the creation and the evolution of mankind, especially in an age of "Progress." Progress: the whole idea and meaning and sound of the word was in accord with the perhaps somewhat less dynamic but also more "scientific" word of Evolution. What Darwin (and his colleagues and followers) did not see was that his very theory about human nature and its origins was a result (and, around 1860, a more or less predictable result) of the evolution of human consciousness (again: Science being part of history, and not the other way around).

There have been several cogent (and other not so cogent) attacks on Darwinist theory (and it is only a theory) during the past 140 years: critics finding evidence here and there to the effect that the process of Natural Selection is not leakproof. I am not a biologist and cannot summarize them here. What I question is one of the basic and near-mechanistic elements of Darwinism: that characteristics acquired by an individual human being cannot be inherited. For the debates about what is "inherited" and what is "acquired" often miss the issue, which is — especially when it comes to human beings — what characteristics are. Human "characteristics" are both inherited and acquired. There are umpteen evidences of this human potentiality (again involving, more often, the intrusion of mind into matter); many more than in the zoological world (even though there, too, critics of Darwin have found some of them). In Chapter 1 of this book I suggested another fundamental limitation of Darwinism, which is the application of Evolution ever further and further backward, claiming that humans may have existed as early as one million years ago. That is a prime example of how unreason lies buried at the bottom of any and every materialist interpretation of mankind, because of its thesis of matter preceding human mind, with mind gradually appearing: when? perhaps in dribs and drabs, much later. (I happen to believe that there is no such thing as "pre-historic" man, historicity being the fourth dimension of human existence from the beginning.) But perhaps the essential fault of Darwinism is its implicit denial that there is any fundamental difference, no matter how physically slight, between human beings and all other living beings. One need not be a religious believer to struggle against this: for if there is really no essential difference between human beings and all other living creatures, then there is no reason to have laws and institutions and mores prohibiting certain human acts and protecting human dignity, indeed, human lives.

I now come to Karl Marx, who is the only one among the four prophets whose reputation has sunk to a low. I do not regret this; I have excoriated what I saw as the basic failures of Marxist thought many times in many of my writings during more than fifty years. But I will not kick a man when he is down. And, as in so many other examples of intellectual commerce, I find the present contemptuous dismissal of Marx opportunistic and fashionable and superficial. It is all due to the obvious failure of Communism in Russia and elsewhere — even though what was happening in Stalin's Russia, and in the institutions and the habits of the Russian people, including millions of Communist Party members, had little or nearly nothing to do with Marx and with his philosophy. Again, this is not the place to list the many misconceptions and failures of that philosophy. Marx, too, was a product of his times: a materialist. (In 1860 Marx claimed that he was the Darwin of Economics.) And while it is to Marx's credit that he was concerned with the, so often and so wrongly exploited, poor working people of his time, the fundamental mistake of his system (besides the condition that *any* system of history is nothing but an abstract structure — that is, largely, nonsensical) was his belief in Economic Man.

However, in this brief running comment I wish to draw attention but to two, perhaps seldom noticed, shortcomings of Marx, germane as these are to my main concern. One is Marx's total neglect of the rising, and most forceful political phenomenon of his time (as it is in ours too), which is nationalism. He consistently thought and wrote about the state, almost never about the nation. He did not realize that nationalism was (and is) different from old-fashioned patriotism, that the very framework of states was changing, that nations and national sentiments were beginning to fill up the framework of states, and that soon not rulers or ruling classes but entire nations would rush at each other. As early as 1914 Marxism failed everywhere: International Socialism melted away in the heat of nationalist emotions like a cold pat of margarine in a hot skillet. By 1914 it was already evident that a British or a French capitalist or industrialist had at least as much in common with his workers as with his German or Austrian capitalist or industrialist counterparts, and so had the respective workers. I am mentioning this to emphasize that nationalism, unlike socialism, is an outcome of sentiments and ideas rather than of economic interests; of inclinations rather than of calculations; a matter of mind rather than of matter — whence its power and attraction.

Another central portion of the Marxian structure — indeed, of the Marxian philosophy of history — was his idea of the Accumulation of Capital, whereby the big fish would eat up the little fish, especially in the last critical stage of the capitalist phase of history. Had Marx only considered something more evident (and insidious): the Accumulation of Opinions — which is, again, a matter of mind and not of matter, involving not a manipulation of masses of monies but of masses of minds, part and parcel of the age of popular sovereignty. It was an accumulation of opinions that made Hitler the chancellor of Germany, and soon the most popular and powerful leader in the history of the German people, just as it is the accumulation of opinions that governs, if not decides, every election — indeed, the history of most democracies.

At this time the reputation of Sigmund Freud has begun to become nicked, though not tattered to the extent of that of Marx. It must be said to Freud's credit that he was less a prototypical thinker of his times than was Darwin, except for two things (and who is not a man of his times at least to some extent?). He also saw himself as a scientist, and he lived in the middle of the, often neurotic, atmosphere of bourgeois Vienna. Again it is not my present purpose, or province, to sum up the main thesis of Freud for which he has been, here and there, criticized: for his overwhelming emphasis on, indeed, for his categorical assertion of the prime sexual motive of human life (especially at the time of infancy). To me, two other, and probably even more basic, shortcomings of Freudianism are (a) his determinism; (b) his insufficient interest in the functions of conscious thinking. Like Darwin and Marx and Einstein, Freud was, and remained, alas, a determinist, a believer in the — essentially primitive — workings of mechanical causality. For him the same causes produced the same effects, in any human mind as well as in any engine — in spite of the myriad instances and

evidences of how the intrusion of mind disturbs and compli-
cates any seemingly, but only seemingly, logical cause-and-effect
relationship.[27] But a more serious shortcoming of Freud and of
his various successors is their emphasis on the subconscious.
Yes: our minds and our lives are influenced, and sometimes
even governed, by actualities and potentialities of which we are
not fully, or even not at all, conscious. But *un*consciousness is
not necessarily *sub*consciousness; and, *contra* Freud, the "subconscious," suggesting depth (there *is* a Germanic inclination to
emphasize depths of thought), is not necessarily the real and
the truest substance of our minds and of our lives, against which
"civilization" (Freud's "super-ego") struggles or must struggle.
The problem of our acts and words and thoughts are problems
of our conscious minds; most of people's troubles are the results
of the inclinations and the habits and the results of their conscious thinking. Perhaps especially in a world where most occupations, including the most mechanical and primitive ones,
are mental and not physical — we have now arrived at a stage of
history where we must begin to think about thinking. And
about the actual act of thinking (which of course involves not
only the act but its habits and its choices) Freud tells us nothing.

We are responsible for what we think — because we choose
our thoughts. Consciousness includes intentionality. It contains

27. In this respect it is not Freud's contemporary adversaries Alfred Adler
and Carl Jung but the younger and most impressive Viktor Frankl who
made the greatest and most important step ahead of Freudianism in psy-
chiatry, the basis of Frankl's "logotherapy" being an emphasis on meaning
and aims of life — in one word, again, the pull of the future, rather than a
push of the past: that is, anti-determinist in its essence.

intentionality (as, for example, there is more to seeing than meets the eye; and both sensory and non-sensory perception contain a perception of meaning). It is increasingly evident — again, especially because of the rapid increase of mental and not physical occupations — that large numbers of people nowadays demonstrate their failing ability to pay attention (including their failure to listen). (And what does attention have to do with the "subconscious"? nothing.[28])

The recognition of the increasing importance of conscious thinking is (or, rather, should be) a recognizable mark of the evolution of human consciousness. Paul Valéry: "If civilized man thinks in quite a different way from primitive man, it is due to the predominance in him of conscious reactions over unconscious products. Of course the latter are indispensable, and sometimes most valuable, substances of our thoughts, but their lasting value depends in the end on our consciousness."[29] Rose Macaulay inveighed against people who constantly use the words "I feel that . . . ": "The advantage that the conscious must always have over the unconscious, the advantage, if it be one, that is perhaps the main difference between sophisticated and primitive forms of life." Thinking, wrote Owen Barfield, "permeates the whole world and indeed the whole universe." It is not the result of the brain "but uses that organ to develop and

28. Simone Weil: "In the intellectual order, the virtue of humility is nothing more nor less than the power of attention." Two centuries earlier, Sir Joshua Reynolds: "A provision of endless apparatus, a bustle of infinite inquiry or research, may be employed to evade and shuffle off real labor — the labor of thinking."
29. Paul Valéry, *The Outlook for Intelligence*, Princeton, 1989, p. 159.

advance the intellect. . . . Only by imagination therefore can the world be known. And what is needed is not only that larger and larger telescopes and more and more sensitive calipers be constructed, but that the human mind should become increasingly aware of its own creative activity."[30]

On 31 December 1999 *Time* magazine declared Albert Einstein to have been the Greatest Man of the Twentieth Century.[31] I am not a physicist, and I cannot refer to experiments (there exist a few) that cast a doubt on Einstein's theory of relativity. But I must attempt to draw attention to some of the limitations of Einstein's Science — or more precisely to his view of reality and of the universe and of man's knowledge of them — which is, after all, what "Science" ought to be about. To begin with, Einstein's famous formula had its forerunners. In 1855 Ludwig (not Georg) Büchner, in *Kraft und Stoff* ("Force and Matter") wrote: "Force means matter and matter force" — that is: $E = mc^2$.[32] A

30. Owen Barfield, *Poetic Diction: A Study in Meaning,* London, 1928, p. 24.
31. Such encomia have not been rare. George Steiner in the *New Yorker* (1994): "What has been the most splendid moment in the history of the human mind? The date of the composition of the Book of Job? The supper during which Socrates expounded the nature of love? The afternoon on which Shakespeare drafted the third and fourth acts of 'King Lear'? On which Schubert sketched the slow movement of his posthumous string quartet? Isaac Newton under that apple tree? No doubt a silly question. Yet a guess, perhaps not altogether silly, does suggest itself. The place: Berne. The exact dates: between March 17 and September 27, 1905. Four papers, mailed and promptly published in the scientific journal *Annalen der Physik,* by a young examiner at the Swiss Patent Office . . . "
32. I cannot refrain from adding this whimsical footnote from *Historical Consciousness,* p. 315.
"Moment is the product of the mass into velocity. To discuss this subject

few years before Einstein's 1905 thesis (which *was* an intuitive and illuminating one) signs had begun to accumulate that cast doubt on the Newtonian classic and static concept of matter and of the physical laws of the universe.[33] People such as Marie Curie (whom Einstein dismissed) discovered a new element, radium, the essence of which was *not* static, radiating constantly. Planck's discovery of energy pulsating not regularly but in "quanta" jumps was another break in the Newtonian system, as he exclaimed in 1900 to his son.

Einstein's important contribution in 1905 was really that of the relativity of simultaneity: speed dependent on different situations in time. But there are other questions about Einstein's famous formula that I dare at least mention. According to Einstein there can be no speed greater than the speed of light.[34] But the speed of light is an imaginary absolute in a vacuum; the speed of light varies in transparent matter, dependent on the refrangibility of the medium; and energy itself is a potentiality that *eventually* becomes an actuality. Also, contrary

---

fully, would lead us too far into the subject Vis Viva, and we must content ourselves with mentioning the fact that *no moment is ever lost, by fully enlightened* Particles. It is scarcely necessary to quote the well-known passage: 'Every moment, that can be snatched from academical duties, is devoted to furthering the cause of the popular Chancellor of the Exchequer. (Clarendon, "History of the Great Rebellion.") A COUPLE consists of a moving particle, raised to the degree M. A., and combined with what is technically called a 'better half.'" [Etc., etc.; italics in the original.] In Lewis Carroll's arch-funny *The Dynamics of a Parti-Cle,* (Oxford, 1865).

33. And wasn't there something very bourgeois in the satisfying sense that something important has proved to be static and, therefore, safe?

34. If there can be no speed greater than the speed of light, hence the relativity of matter? No: hence the relativity of human knowledge.

to general belief, Einstein's theory of relativity had little to do with the actual production of nuclear fission and then of nuclear power. For the purposes of this essay this does not matter. What matter are the self-imposed (that is, conscious) limitations of Einstein's thinking. Like Darwin, Marx, Freud, he was a determinist and remained so.[35] He was unwilling — unwilling, rather than unable — to accept Heisenberg's discoveries and their meaning. Consequently, the last thirty years of Einstein's life were infertile, punctuated by his occasional stumbling attempts to deny Indeterminacy, all of them vain. Of course, no man ought to be blamed because of the decline of his mental powers at or after a certain age. But what was wrong, and remained wrong, was Einstein's view of reality. "Physics," he said in 1925, "is an attempt conceptually to grasp reality." No, said Niels Bohr: "It is wrong to think that the task of physics is to find out how nature is. Physics concerns what we can say about nature." Again, Einstein: "Physical reality exists, and it would exist even if there were no observers to observe it." No, said Schrödinger:

35. "Quantum theory and general relativity, each brilliantly successful in its own domain, rest on very different principles and give highly divergent pictures of nature. According to general relativity, the world is deterministic, the fundamental equations of nature are nonlinear, and the correct picture of nature is at bottom, geometric. According to quantum theory, there is an intrinsic randomness in nature, its fundamental equations are linear, and the correct language in which to describe nature seems to be closer to abstract algebra than to geometry." Adrian Kent, "Night thoughts of a quantum physicist," in *Series A, Mathematical, Physical and Engineering Sciences,* London, Royal Society, 1996, p. 77. Well . . . Also, p. 76: "The great discoveries of 20th-century physics have sunk so deeply into the general consciousness[?] that it now takes an effort of will to stand back and try to see them afresh." Not necessarily.

"The world is a construction of our perception, of our sensations, of our memories." "Leaving out everything subjective," Einstein once declared, was "the supreme aim of my thought." He could not liberate himself from the, increasingly senseless, subjective/objective antithesis; he could not accept the unavoidable element (and limitation) of personal participation. He often asserted his belief in God, but in a very strange way: "Morality is of the highest importance—but for us, not for God." "I believe in Spinoza's God who reveals himself in the orderly harmony of what exists, not in a God who concerns himself with the destiny and actions of human beings." So much —I once wrote—for Einstein the humanist. Perhaps this was too harsh a dismissal. But we ought nonetheless to recognize that the title of the Greatest Man of the Twentieth Century (not to speak of the greatest mind of all times) ought not to be bestowed on a man who, at the end of the Modern Age, could not free his mind from the axioms of Spinoza and Descartes, at the beginning of the Modern Age, nearly four hundred years ago.[36]

Yet despite the shortcomings of his philosophy Einstein deserves our respect. While it is a symptom of the intellectual stagnation (and confusion) at the end of an age that "modern"

36. Albert Einstein, *Autobiographical Notes,* Carbondale, Ill., 1991, p. 11: "the objects with which geometry is concerned seems to be of no different type from the objects of sensory perception." P. 77: "Physics is an attempt conceptually to grasp reality as something that is considered to be independent of its being observed. In this sense one speaks of 'physical reality.'" Earlier about his youth: " . . . a first attempt to free myself from the chains of the 'merely personal.' . . . Out yonder there was this huge world, which exists independently of us human beings."

statements of antiquated ideas are treated with great respect, other — also antiquated — crude attempts are made to reject "modernity" altogether. A repugnant and disturbing example was represented by those German savants (Lenard and Stark) who rejected relativity theory because of Einstein's Jewishness; or by those American fundamentalists who rejected Darwinism because of their profession of a "creationism" that is both confused and rigid, the worst possible combination. We may be moving into a barbarian age when the craziest myths may become popular among hundreds of millions. Compared to such myths we must give Darwin, Marx, Freud, Einstein their due. They were men of their time; they were part of its history; they have been part of our history too. But, near the end of the Modern Age, they were neither prophets nor the greatest of its minds.

One hundred and fifty years ago the German radical Feuerbach wrote: "The old world made spirit parent of matter. The new makes matter parent of spirit." That is as good a summation of the historical philosophy of materialism as any. (Like his contemporary and friend Ludwig Büchner, a pithy forerunner of Einstein [of sorts], Feuerbach foreran Darwin and even Marx of *Das Kapital*.) ("Men of letters," wrote the Scottish mystical poet Alexander Smith in *Dreamthorp* [1863] "forerun science as the morning star the dawn.") One hundred and fifty years later the overwhelming majority of scientists as well as computer designers and propagators see not only the world but the future of the world in accord with Feuerbach's maxim. They are wrong. We, around the year 2000, are (or, rather, should be) well ahead with the recognition that matter — as we knew it, as we know it, and as we will know it — is increasingly dependent on spirit; or that the human mind, with its main instrument, the inner and outer eye, with its miraculous powers and also with its existential limitations, both precedes and defines the characteristics of matter.

The materialistic philosophy and theories of the nineteenth century were hardly more than one chapter in the history of Science, even though its consequences are still all around us, blocking our vision. Physics has ended by explaining away matter itself, leaving us with an ever increasing skeleton, a more complex but essentially empty scaffolding of abstract mathematical formulae. Meanwhile evidences accumulate of the intrusion of mind into "matter." We need not hack our way through the verbal jungle of "post-modern" philosophers of the twentieth century, even while we recognize their, long overdue, rejection of Objectivism. Unfortunately for so many of them this means but a supermodern kind of Subjectivism, which is a very insufficient approximation of the reality that the key to the universe is mind, not matter.

Not only the evolution of our medical knowledge but the very history, the etiology (meaning: the study of the origins) of illnesses, especially among the so-called advanced peoples of the modern world, indicates the — sometimes palpable, but in essence deep and ever mysterious — confluences of mind and matter, indeed, of mind *preceding* matter. An illustration of this cannot belong in this small book, with its considerable limitations.

Still, I must insist that the very recognition of these conditions is in itself evolutionary — not in the Darwinian sense but in the sense of the evolution of our consciousness. One of my favorite illustrations of this involves not philosophy or physics or medical anthropology but the modern history of Switzerland. That country was among the poorest in Western Europe in the eighteenth century, mainly because of the then accepted belief that mountains were horrid; they were hated and feared; to be avoided in every way. And then, as Owen Barfield wrote, "The economic and social structure of Switzerland [became] noticeably affected by the tourist industry and that [was] due only in part to increasing facilities of travel. It was no less due to the condition that the *mountains* that twentieth-century man sees are not the mountains that eighteenth-century man saw."[37]

The materialist explanations of the world and of human nature have been — at least for some time — made easily adaptable to a mass democratic age, partly because of the increasingly primitive conditions of public discourse and speech. To this we must add the vested interests of the materialist philosophies espoused not only by scientists but by many other writers and scholars. One such example is the Viennese Karl R. Popper (whose *Open Society* has been praised, among others, by the British Prime Minister Margaret Thatcher and the well-known international financier George Soros, who wrote that Popper

---

37. Or in other words: the attraction and the consequent prosperity of Switzerland was greatly due to the visions of the English Lake Poets and of other romantics. (The doctors followed; mountain air that was perilous and even lethal in the eighteenth century became salubrious and health-giving in the nineteenth.)

provided the greatest intellectual influence in his life). "The surest path to intellectual perdition," Popper wrote, is "the abandonment of real problems for the sake of verbal problems." "Never let yourself be goaded into taking seriously problems about words and their meanings. What we must take seriously are questions of fact, and assertions about facts: theories and not hypotheses; the problems they solve; and the problems they raise." (And are these not stated in words?) "Much of my work in recent years has been in defense of objectivity.... One cannot speak of anything like correspondence between a statement and a fact.... There seems to be no prospect of explaining the correspondence of a statement to a fact."[38]

This is nonsense, because "facts" do not exist by themselves — surely not in our minds. There is no such thing as an entirely independent, or isolated, or unchanging fact. Any "fact" is inseparable from our association of it with another "fact" (and in our minds this association is necessarily an association with a *preceding* fact). Any "fact" that is beyond or beneath our cognition, or consciousness, or perception, is meaningless to us — which is why we must be very careful not to dissociate "facts" from the way in which they are stated. Every "fact" is not only dependent on but inseparable from our statement of it. We must never consider a "fact" apart from its meaning to us or apart from the expression of its meaning. And statement means speech, and speech consists of words which are matters of meanings. We cannot speak, or even think, about

38. Karl L. Popper, *Unended Quest: An Intellectual Autobiography,* London, 1982, pp. 19, 138, 140.

anything of which the existence is entirely meaningless — that is, unknown — to us.

Allow me to illustrate this through an argument with a dear and good friend of mine. He said: "There stood a magnolia tree in the front garden of 17 Ennerdale Road. In 1997 it was cut down, so that it is no longer there. Isn't that a fact?" Yes: but only (1) because of the present usage of the word "fact"; (2) because of its inseparability from its associations. About (1): my *OED* states that "fact," deriving from the Latin "factum" (that is: something made) replaced "feat" in English about 1500. (Thus before 1500 that "fact" was perhaps a "feat" but not a "fact" — thereafter, and especially during the past two hundred years, we have unduly extended and applied the usage of the word.)[39] But more important is (2): that "facts" are inevitably dependent on our associations of them. "Magnolia," "tree," "front garden," "Ennerdale Road," "1997" are not merely the packaging of the above-mentioned fact. They are part and parcel of that particular "fact" itself. Once you remove "magnolia,"

39. Peter Burke, *Vico,* Oxford, 1985, p. 23: Vico "attempted . . . to reconstruct the beliefs of the early philosophers of Italy on the basis of the etymology of certain Latin words. For example, he related the word *fatum,* 'fate,' to *factum,* 'made,' and also to *fatus est,* 'he spoke,' arguing that the Italian philosophers must have thought that fate was inexorable because 'created things are God's word' and 'what is made cannot be unmade.'" Jacques Barzun, *Begin Here: The Forgotten Conditions of Teaching and Learning,* Chicago, 1991, p. 176: "To modern faith, figures denote fact, whereas words are opinion — as if opinion were not a fact, too, and the figures often a guess." Owen Barfield, *The Rediscovery of Meaning and Other Essays,* Middletown, Conn., 1977, pp. 132–133: "Words are only themselves by being more than themselves. Perhaps the same thing is true of human beings."

"Ennerdale Road," "1997" from the above statement, the "fact" is reduced to the mere absence of a tree. That "fact" then is no longer what it was.[40]

Any recognition of the great and mysterious functions of the mind is different from the recognition of brainpower. The intellectualization of life, the arranging of people and their thoughts and their experiences into abstract intellectual categories is always imperfect. The intrusion of thinking into the structure of events may be good or bad. But the conscious recognition of this intrusion cannot be but good in the long run.

In 1749 Julien Offroy de la Mettrie published *L'Homme machine,* Man as a Machine. Wrong as de la Mettrie was, that was *at that time* a forward step of sorts: a reaction against religious dogmas and doctrines involving human nature, the appeal of which seemed to be drying up. Now, wrote de la Mettrie (a view with which the majority of the French encyclopedists tended to agree), now that we have learned more and more about the physical world (that is, about mechanical causality), it is high time to apply such a method of knowledge to the human being itself: admittedly a very complex machine, perhaps the most complex machine we know, but a machine nonetheless. And 250 years later this is what people who believe in computers or in "Artificial Intelligence" think.[41] Two hundred

---

40. What I mean by association Goethe meant by "theory": "Let the facts themselves speak for their theory. . . . Don't look for anything behind the phenomena; they themselves are the theory. . . . The greatest achievement would be to understand that everything factual is already its own theory."
41. In the new republic of the United States "the invention of a machine or the improvement of an implement is of more importance than a master-

and fifty years out of date: they think that brain is mind, which it is not. Mechanical or artificial "brains" may one day be cobbled together. But a mechanical mind is an oxymoron. Let me add a flat sentence to Pascal's immortal maxim ("the heart has reasons which reason does not know"): the mind has functions that the brain hardly knows.[42]

It may be argued that "mind" and "brain" are semantic distinctions. This is not the place to refute such an argument, but it *is* the place to argue something provable and telling: that, whether "mind" or "brain," its functions do *not* follow the "laws" of natural science of physics. One example (a proof, too, of the dependence of "facts" on their associations). When a box or a sack or any vessel is full, it is evidently more and more difficult to stuff more things into it. But the *more* we know something the *easier* it is to remember and to fit in new matter — as, for instance, a name or a number or a date that reminds us (note the very word: *re-minds*) of something that we already know.[43] This brings us to the — again — unphysical — distinction

---

piece of Raphael." Thus de la Mettrie's contemporary Benjamin Franklin, Self-Made Man and Thinker.

42. Note the difference between Pascal and Freud, since according to the latter, the "heart" (or, in his terminology, the subconscious mind) is irrational. (Freud's contemporary the Austrian writer Robert Musil is closer to Pascal: "We do not have too much intellect and too little soul, but too little intellect in matters of the soul.")

43. E.g., a telephone number or a house number identical to our birth-date; or, say, 1776.

Here is another example of how the functioning human mind does not accord with the laws of physics: while it is easier to wrestle with a weak body than with a strong one, it is more difficult to wrestle with a weak mind than with a strong one.

between knowledge and understanding. Again I invoke Pascal, who said: "We understand more than we know." This seems, at first, utterly illogical. Isn't "understanding" a synthesis: a further, and better, result of accumulated and well-digested knowledge? Sometimes, yes; but in innumerable other instances, no. A glimpse of intuitive understanding may precede, rather than follow, knowledge—especially when it comes to the perceptions and relations of human beings to other human beings. And when it comes to such perceptions and relations—which are, essentially, *the* most important relationships of our entire lives—whether it precedes knowledge or not, understanding is more important than is certainty.

It involves the *participation*—or more precisely: an attempt at participation—of one human being in another.[44] With this sense, or meaning, of participant understanding the antiseptic, or wholly detached, ideal of objectivity disappears. And the primacy of certainty (or of accuracy), too: because this participation is always, and necessarily, incomplete. No human being understands (or even knows) another human being entirely, or completely, or certainly, or even accurately. But this is no reason to despair. To the contrary: it is this very incompleteness—or uncertainty; or inaccuracy—that gives both meaning and charm to human relationships. What A says to B is not exactly what B hears him say—mostly because of the great variety of B's already existing associations.[45] Human "communications,"

---

44. This sense of participation, including physical participation, is what the phrase "carnal knowledge" meant centuries ago.
45. This *added* meaning and charm exists too, in our knowledge of other languages. To understand another language well means more than a knowl-

unlike mechanical communications and causalities, are necessarily incomplete, nay, inaccurate — unlike the relations of numbers. Numbers are static and fixed and unchanging; life is not.[46] *Numbers: The Language of Science* — a cliché, and the title of a book. They are not the language of human beings. We ought perhaps not go as far as Kierkegaard who wrote 150 years ago that "numbers are the negation of truth." (The Italian poet Eugenio Montale 130 years later: "Today this negation has become an intoxicating collective pseudo-truth.") It is sufficient for us to recognize that understanding is of a higher order than accuracy. Measurement depends on numbers. Its aim is accuracy. But understanding, including imagination, is immune to measurement (and imagination may be immune even to neurological experimentation). Numbers are devoid of wisdom: to give them meaning, to reconcile them with life, we have to think about them and clothe them in words. To Galileo quantities were everything: "I think that tastes, odors, colors, and so forth,

---

edge of its vocabulary. It also means the understanding of the different shades of nuances of some of its expressions, beyond their dictionary equivalences: for example, that the French "honneur" means something slightly different from the English "honor," despite their common Latin origins ("an honest man," "un homme honnête"). There is charm and pleasure in recognizing such things — as it is to relish a customary particular lilt of a phrase on the tongue of a lovable person.

46. I.e., a half-truth is not a 50 percent truth but a 100 percent truth and a 100 percent untruth compounded together. In mathematics 100 plus 100 makes 200. In human life it makes *another kind* of a 100. In our lives, that is, minds, there are soft hundreds and hard hundreds, warm hundreds and cold hundreds, red hundreds and green hundreds, hundreds that are growing and hundreds that are shrinking. In sum, they are neither stationary nor fixed.

are no more than mere names. They reside only in the consciousness."[47] (This is, interestingly, subjectivism even more
than it is materialism.) Three centuries later Simone Weil
wrote: "But in applying analysis to physics there is a risk that
what legitimates it may be forgotten. It is only in geometry and
mechanics that algebra has significance."[48]

Plato may have been the first man who invented — that is, he
was the first who consciously recognized and therefore needed
to express — the word *quality* ("poiotes": Cicero translated it
into "qualitas" from "qualis"), which is something which computers, with their nearly incredible capacity to manipulate quantities, are incapable even to ascertain, let alone "know" or "understand." What I wrote in the first paragraph of this chapter —
"What kind of a man is A.?" — rarely refers to anything but to the
quality of his character, that is, to his mind. Quality is inherent
in, indeed, it marks ("qualifies") every human act and thought
and expression. Computers store and transmit information. In
order to do that they must classify the elements of information;
and classification necessarily reduces, if not eliminates, qualities
and their nuances. Classification necessitates categorization and
leads to homogenization, whereby qualities and even differences
become dependent on their preconceived and programmed
categories.

In this respect consider the extraordinarily acute and very
important distinction made by Owen Barfield: "Confused as
they are now in most people's minds, equality and uniformity

47. *Discoveries and Opinions of Galileo,* New York, 1957, p. 274.
48. Simone Weil, *Gravity and Grace,* London, 1987, p. 139.

are two entirely different principles, and the demands for them are differently motivated. . . . Whereas the idea of equality is rooted in the strength of the superpersonal idea of justice, the demand for uniformity is rooted in the meanness of the personal sting of envy."[49] This has a meaning well beyond computers. It is deeply relevant to society and politics.

Computers cannot participate, except perhaps with each other. And participation, with all of its inaccuracies, depends on listening — which, in turn, requires attention: and concentration.[50]

The nature — and the essence — of scientific and mathematical thinking requires categories; yet human life and the human mind are governed by tendencies rather than by categories. Example: what we mean by national characteristics — which are historic rather than racial in their origins — we mean nothing less or nothing more than national tendencies. Categories are actualities, on which science must absolutely depend in its experiments; but life and history demonstrate, again and again, the existence of potentialities (which are, more often than not, the sources of actualities). The very quality of a historical description may depend on its suggestion of a potentiality: the description of a choice, or of a contingency at a certain time, and of a suggestion of its potential consequences. Meanwhile Heisenberg's discoveries brought potentiality back into the causalities of physics; and what are "polls" but attempts to ascertain potentialities eventually becoming actualities? Signifi-

49. Barfield, *The Rediscovery of Meaning and Other Essays,* p. 211.
50. Miguel de Unamuno, *The Tragic Sense of Life,* p. 237: "For while spirit tends towards concentration, material energy tends toward diffusion."

cance, too, is related both to tendency and potentiality. These are not semantic categories, not definitions but distinctions. The ability to recognize distinctions is one of the most essential capacities of the human mind, not to speak of the qualities of art. There is the distinction, nowadays so rarely recognized or cultivated, whether in sexual inclinations or in art, between imagination and fantasy: the former, though coming from the innermost self, still respectful of reality, the latter not.

I wrote "respectful of reality" (which of course is *not* entirely outside of and independent of us) — which is why idealism and realism are not opposites. The intelligent idealist is at the same time a realist. He understands the primacy of mind over matter; but he recognizes matter, indeed he must be grateful to it — or to God — for it. A friar once said to the fifteenth-century German mystic Meister Eckhart: "I wish I had your soul in my body." Eckhart said: "That would be useless. A soul can save itself only in its own appointed body." A German poet once wrote: "I have a great awe of the human body, for the soul is inside it." And there are as great and grave dangers in categorical idealism as there are in categorical materialism. There is the — often German, but also Russian — tendency, or belief, in an idealistic determinism. What matters is not what ideas do to men but what men do to their ideas; how and when they choose them, and how and why they accommodate them to their own wishes, interests, lives, circumstances. Wrong in this sense, too, was the English "idealist" historian and thinker R. C. Collingwood (sometimes referred to as a prophet of post-modernism), who wrote that history is nothing but the history of ideas. What we must keep in mind is not only that no idea exists without the human being who thinks it and represents it, but also that no idealism exists in the abstract, that every philosophy of idealism is also — and inevitably — a historical phenomenon.[51]

There is a distinction between a merely anti-materialist idealism and a realistic idealism that encompasses the coexistence (and confluence) of matter and spirit. This was what Jakob Burckhardt meant, more than 130 years ago, when he said that "if happiness is to be found in our misfortunes, it can only be a spiritual one: to be turned facing the past so as to save the culture of former times, and facing the future so as to give an

51. *Historical Consciousness*, p. 152: "There are . . . all kinds of dangers inherent in the tendency to take ideas *too* seriously. When, for example, Professor [Michael] Oakeshott says that 'history is the historian's experience. It is "made" by nobody save the historian: to write history is the only way of making it.' I understand what he means; but I know, too, that he is separating the idea of history from history; or, in other words, he is distinguishing between the past and the reconstruction of the past in the historian's mind which, according to him, alone is 'history.' In spite of my deep-seated sympathy with much of the neo-idealist position, it is this separation of 'the past' from 'history' which I cannot accept." (There is, namely, an implicit contradiction between Oakeshott's statement and Collingwood's statement to the effect that the past is dead but "in some sense is still living in the present. This is very true: it is only that the presence of the past in the world and in our lives is something that is both more widespread and deeper than the process of reconstruction which goes on in the historian's mind."

Romano Guardini in *The Dissolution (End) of the Modern World*, Wilmington, Del., 1998, pp. 79–80: Man is not "the creature that idealism makes of him. Although idealism espouses the spiritual, it equates the human with the absolute spirit. . . . Consequently, he possesses no freedom in any forthright sense, nor does he truly carve his destiny into an initiative proper to himself. . . . Man may be finite, but he is also a real person — irreplaceable in his unique act of being — one whose dignity cannot be supplanted, whose responsibility cannot be avoided."

example of the spiritual in an age which might otherwise succumb entirely to the material." To this inspiring and moving statement I now add that 130 years later it may only seem that people are succumbing entirely to the material. Indeed the danger may arise from elsewhere: from false idealisms and fake spiritualisms of many kinds — from a spiritual thirst or hunger that arises at the end of an age, and that materialism cannot satisfy.

FOUR
An Illustration

✦

1959. • The limits of knowledge. • The limits
of objectivity. • The limits of definitions.
• The limits of mathematics. • The inevitability of
relationships. • Inevitable unpredictability.
• Insufficient materialism. • The limits of idealism.

Again — and for the last time — I must begin a chapter with a personal account.[1]

Readers who have followed my chapters until now may think that this book is the work of a, probably idiosyncratic, philosophical thinker, rather than a historian. This is not so. Nineteen of my twenty-one published books, the results of more than fifty years of historical writing, are narrative histories. *This* writer and *this* thinker (or, if you prefer: this historian and this philosopher) consist within the

---

1. On the chapter title: Illustration (*OED*), "The action or fact of illustrating." Originally: lighting up, enlightenment, once spiritual rather than intellectual. "The action of making or fact of being illustrious, brilliant, or distinguished." This is not my purpose. It is, rather (*OED* 3): "To make clear or evident to the mind; setting forth clearly or pictorially; elucidation, explanation, exemplification" — in this case, historically. This is close to *illative:* "introducing or stating an inference."

same person. My concerns with how to write history and with how to think about history have never been separate but always allied. They have been reflected, and even exemplified, in every book of mine, no matter how different their themes or topics have been.

As much as I thought it possible, I have consistently tried to apply my convictions about the hierarchy of historical factors (perhaps presumptuously: my perspective of human nature) in a successive series of my books. My conviction of the primacy of mind over matter — that what is important is what people think and believe and that the entire material and institutional organization of the world is largely a superstructure of that — was suggested and, here and there stated, in my earliest books. But when, during the fourth decade of my life, my ideas about the relative hierarchy of historical factors were crystallizing sufficiently to have written the first draft of a chapter of *Historical Consciousness,* sometime in late 1959 a sudden and anxious thought floated up to the surface of my mind. What is the use of all such propositions if they are bereft of their applications?[2] They ought to be applied and illustrated by concrete — meaning: real, historical — examples. *Primo vivere, deinde philosophari.* Then I wrote out, on a sheet of paper, the plan for a small book dealing with American-Russian relations. My publishers took up the plan. *A History of the Cold War* consisted of

2. This recognition may have had something to do with an, often disguised, blessing in my career: that I was not only a writer but a teacher of history *and* — this is important — a teacher of undergraduates, to whom I had to try to speak about large and complex topics as clearly and as briefly as I could, yet without superficiality.

two parts. The first half of the book was a narrative survey of American-Russian relations from 1763 to 1959. The titles of the chapters of the second half ("The Two Peoples: The tendencies of their societies"; "The Two Societies: The tendencies of their political theories"; "The Two States: The development of their national interests"; "The Two Nations: The development of their national character"; "Conclusion: The great historical movements of our times") ought to show the structure of the book, illustrating my above-mentioned sequential hierarchy of historical factors. I employed the same construction, suggesting the same division and the same hierarchy, in many other books of mine, notably in *The Last European War, 1939–1941* ("Part I. The Main Events." "Part II. The Main Movements. 1. The lives of the peoples. 2. The march of the armies. 3. The movements of politics. 4. The relations of states. 5. The sentiments of nations. 6. The convergences of thought and of belief.") And also in others, including *Outgrowing Democracy: A History of the United States in the 20th Century.*

It will be seen that this structure: narrative summary first, followed by analytical chapters on successive levels, is particularly applicable to large topics.

But besides this decision to illustrate my beliefs about the relative hierarchy of historical factors there occurred another, perhaps even more important, event in the history of my interests around that time.[3] My readers may recall from the previous chapter my recognition of the illusions of unquestionable Ob-

---

3. A history of one's interests, while not separable from, is something else than an autobiography, and even than an intellectual autobiography.

jectivity, and my skepticism about the unquestioned applicability of the Scientific Method to History. Yet I still believed in
the existence of two separate forms of thought, the scientific and
the historical, and that was that. (I did believe in the primacy
of the second, whereby I thought that C. P. Snow's thesis of
Two Cultures was insufficient.) I had, too, a vague feeling of
suspicion that certain discoveries of twentieth-century science
may have at least suggested some deep-seated questions about
Scientific or Mechanically-Causal or Mathematical Certitude.
However, in 1959 something else happened; in my mind certain
thoughts began to crystallize. These crystallizations were sometimes occasional, sometimes startling; often they were helped
and clarified by what I found during my undisciplined reading.
And that was the recognition that the very knowledge (or, let us
say, the cognition) of physicists about subatomic events — that
is, about the very basic elements of matter — that their recognitions about the inevitable limitations of that kind of cognition,
corresponds, and impressively, to the inevitable limitations of
our historical knowledge: that is, of the knowledge of human
beings about human beings. There was no longer any Duality.
There was no longer any absolute separation of Mind and Matter. The world no longer consisted of Objects and Subjects.
There was no Science without Scientists. There was — there is —
only one kind of human knowledge. Bang!

To this I devoted a chapter (almost entirely unremarked),
"History and Physics," in *Historical Consciousness,* published in
1968 (republished and extended in 1984 and 1995). Ever since
that time I thought that I must extend this chapter, or — more

directly, more tellingly, — illustrate it with an example,[4] apply it to a commonly recognizable historical person or period or problem. Well, the time has come for this. Now.

For the purposes of an illustration (and it is not more than an example), I have chosen the problem of our knowledge of Adolf Hitler, for more than one reason. Some, perhaps many, things about his life will be familiar to my readers. I have thought (and read and written) a fair amount about him, including *The Hitler of History* (1997); and though I do not choose to write or perhaps even read more about Hitler, problematic questions about him have kept surfacing in my mind even since the completion of that book. After all, his appearance in — and effect on — the last century of the Modern Age amount to more than a historical episode (which is what many of his countrymen still prefer to think): it was an event of enormous historical significance.

It is not only that it is not given to any human being to know another human being completely. We have seen that we must also eschew the nineteenth-century ideal, or illusion, about the definiteness or completeness of historical knowledge. One example: we know that Hitler first stated the need for a preliminary planning of a campaign against Russia as early as

4. "History is philosophy, teaching by examples." Dionysius Halicarnassus (and Bolingbroke, nearly two thousand years later).

31 July 1940. That is a "fact," ascertainable from records in the German archives and also from other sources. Now I have argued that no fact is separable from the statement of that fact, which is why I choose my words carefully: for Hitler on 31 July 1940 "stated the need for" the "preliminary planning" (not yet the definitive plan) of the invasion of Russia. But there is more trouble with "fact." It carries within it a sense of definitiveness. And what is interesting — and telling — about this "fact" is that it occurred on 31 July 1940 — that is, even before the German aerial assault on Britain began, and when the planning for an invasion of England was still in the works. It is not only that Hitler's declaration on 31 July 1940 did not yet amount to a definite plan. It is also that Hitler could have decided (and thought) otherwise — an obvious potentiality that sparks our interest, and sharpens our cognition about this remarkable, and at first sight (but only at first sight) unreasonable, decision. In sum, it belongs to that particular "fact."

In any event, we can know what Hitler said or did; but we cannot know, with certainty, exactly what was in his mind at any particular time. He could have thought otherwise; it is quite likely that, while pondering this choice, he was also thinking, at times, otherwise. He was a secretive man, in spite of his volubility and his tendency to overwhelm his hearers with his monologues. He himself emphasized his secretiveness on more than one occasion.[5] This is one of the reasons why those histo-

5. One example: Hitler to Admiral Raeder on 21 May 1939: "I possess three kinds of secrecy: the first, when we talk among ourselves; the second,

rians who stated that the evidence of Hitler's beliefs, plans, and decisions were all there in *Mein Kampf* are wrong. In addition to his secretiveness, Hitler was a believer in the spoken, not in the written, word. We have many evidences of this. He used speech for many purposes, often successfully. What was recorded of what he said, whether officially or unofficially, whether by his followers or by others, is of course part of the historical record. But: did he believe what he was saying? At times, yes; there is some evidence (even physical) that he seems to have been carried away by his own oratory when he spoke. (I write "he seems" — another matter that we cannot state with certainty.)

But there are also many evidences — and crucial ones — that he did not always believe what he was saying. There are two important instances of this. One involves Russia, the other involves Jews — his two basic obsessions, almost all historians say. Until the very last days of his life he made statements about "Jewish Bolshevism." Yet there are many evidences of his admiration for Stalin, including expressions of his awareness that the latter was anti-Semitic. Most interesting — and mysterious[6] — is the occasional duality of his statements (and even decisions) about Jews. In *Mein Kampf* and elsewhere he declared that his realization of the Jewish "pestilence" crystallized in Vienna, between 1908 and 1912. Yet we have evidence that Hitler's fanati-

---

I keep for myself; the third, those are problems about the future about which I must keep thinking." In many other statements Hitler avowed his secretiveness.

6. See Chapter 2, Owen Chadwick: "All historical events remain in part mysterious."

cal anti-Semitism crystallized (if that is the word) much later, in Munich, in the late spring of 1919; that there is no conclusive record of anti-Semitic statements by Hitler before that; that he had Jewish acquaintances in Vienna; that he, on occasion, was an appreciative guest in Jewish houses.[7] Even *after* 1919 we have evidences that he was inclined to protect, or even make favorable references to certain Jews (especially artists); that he allowed Himmler to make contact with certain Jews and allow their departure abroad in the middle of the war; that he apparently not only took care that there be no written record of an order to physically exterminate Jews after 1941 but that he showed no interest in — indeed, he refrained from looking at or reading reports of — their extermination. He knew, of course, and he repeated occasionally, that anti-Semitism was a powerful rhetorical and political and popular instrument. That he had learned in Vienna. But how much did that count in his statements and decisions? How much did his own beliefs weigh in the balance of his actions? Note these words: "Much," "count," "weigh," "balance." These are inadequate words, because they connote quantities. A better phrasing of the question would be: was his Judaeophobia his fundamental obsession? That is more of a qualitative question, and the best this historian can say is: yes and no.

Or: in some ways yes, in some ways no. Or: sometimes yes, sometimes no. Or: probably we will never know. In yet other words: Hitler carried his secret with him into the grave. But

7. Asserted by this writer in *The Hitler of History*, and illustrated magisterially by Brigitte Hamann in *Hitler's Vienna* (1998).

then that is true of every other human being. Only consider: all of these matters, or secrets, are matters of the mind. We can ascertain, relying on medical records, many things about Hitler's physical condition. But when a historian thinks of another human being, his principal interest is with the person's mind, with its workings and effects. And about that he can never say anything with certainty. He is engaged in a mental construction. The original Latin word for "construction" is *fictio* (not *factum:* the *facta* serve the *fictio*).

We are faced with a challenge. But the capacity to think, and to mentally construct; to understand and, yes, to imagine, are the great gifts of human existence. Perhaps, paradoxically, the understanding of the limits of our knowledge of other human beings may actually (and not only potentially) enrich the *quality* of our knowledge — a knowledge that cannot be antiseptic and distant but, on the contrary, need be personal and participant, since it involves a knowledge of the species by the same species (an understanding within which self-knowledge itself is inevitably participant). These are the conditions and the limits of historical knowledge. And they correspond to the very conditions and limits of scientific certitude. We now know that the behavior of a subatomic particle is not always predictable, and that this uncertainty is due not to inadequate precisions of measurement but to a principle that can be demonstrated by experiment. The limits of our knowledge and the conditions of our participation are unavoidable.

More than half a century separates us from Hitler's death. His history and the history of the Third Reich is probably documented as much as anything else in the twentieth century. By now hundreds of books and thousands of studies and articles have been published about him. These published writings reflect the opinions and the inclinations of their authors as a matter of course. There is nothing new in this. Nor is there anything particularly novel in the authors' often selective use of documents, texts, statements, evidence that sustain their views. And in the case of Hitler there may be additional considerations illustrating the illusory nature of Objectivity.

What does it mean (in our time) to be "objective" about Hitler? The old (pre-modern) meaning of "objective" changed through centuries; it was once the opposite of its present meaning; it connoted a connection between the knower or thinker and the subject or aim of his knowing or thinking. The present usage of "objective" suggests that (a) one must not be governed by prejudices; (b) one must recognize, and eventually record, not only Hitler's vices but also his virtues — that is, evidences of his "positive" as well as "negative" qualities. But we do not get very far with this. I myself have written that Hitler "had very considerable intellectual talents. He was also courageous, self-assured, on many occasions steadfast, loyal to his friends and to those working for him, self-disciplined, and modest in his physical wants." But: what this suggests ought not be misconstrued. It does not mean: lo and behold! Hitler was only 50 percent bad. Human nature is not like that.[8] In Germany Hitler is —

---

8. In *The Hitler of History,* pp. 43–44, where I employed my argument (see

still — such a touchy subject that few academic historians state something like the above. More regrettable is the German inclination — understandable, though not justifiable — to separate Hitler from the history of the German people during his period. (An extreme example is Professor Klaus Hildebrand's dictum: "One must not speak of National Socialism but of Hitlerism.") At the same time some German historians have begun to relativize the German past — that is, they pick and choose from the record of World War II, mostly by comparing the brutal deeds of German National Socialism with those of Soviet Communism. (This was their fundamental argument during the "Historikerstreit" of 1986–1987.) They have not yet come to terms with Hitler.

Other German historians have written of the necessity of "objectifying" or "historicizing" the years 1933–1945, Hitler, National Socialism, the Third Reich, instead of "subjectifying" or "demonizing" him or them — a commendable proposition, except that "objectivity" and "historicity" are not the same thing.[9] "Objectivity" requires the desirability of an antisep-

---

Chapter 3, p. 138) about a half-truth not being a 50 percent truth but a mixture of a (100 percent) truth with (a 100 percent) untruth. Consider also La Rochefoucauld: "There are evil men who would be less dangerous if they had no good in them."

9. Professor Andreas Hillgruber: in 1940 Hitler's offers to Britain were "subjectively, honest." What does this mean? Another nationalist, the knowledgeable and "revisionist" historian Rainer Zitelmann: the "subjective" factors in the condemnation of Hitler ought to be dismissed. "We must see things [less simply] but scientifically. The black-and-white pictures are no longer convincing." Does this mean that — especially from an "objective" distance — the image of Hitler must be gray? That is not what Zitelmann seems to mean. He would, I think, agree that because of the

tic separation of the observer from the subject, a narrowing, whereas "historicizing" requires a broadening of perspective. The first means distancing yourself from the "subject," the second attempting to rise above it; the first a detachment from a "place" and from a person, the second possibly a detachment from a "time" but not from a person.

To be "objective" about Hitler is one thing; to attempt to understand him is another; and the second is not at all more exculpatory than the first, perhaps even the contrary. For example: can we expect a Jewish historian to be "objective" about Hitler? (Or, indeed: can we expect anyone to be "objective" about someone who did him harm?) Perhaps not; but we *can* expect him, or indeed anyone, to attempt to understand. But that attempt must depend on the very quality of his participation, including at least a modicum of understanding his own self: the sense that Hitler was, after all, a human being, so that some of his characteristic inclinations were not *entirely* different from those of the person now thinking about him. So, instead of the desideratum of a complete disconnection between the observer and the observed, the effort to a mental participation. And here enters another inevitable condition of place or time. Ten or thirty or sixty years after Hitler's death a Patagonian or a

---

coexistence of good and evil, the composition of human nature may be likened to the coat of a zebra, with black and white stripes in its make up. But what matters is *not* the ratio of black stripes, not their quantity but the quality — and intensity — of their blackness. And in this respect no quantitative (Zitelmann: "scientific") analysis or a meticulous pointillism will do. What *kind* of blackness — a question that transcends scientific or perhaps even artistic analysis.

Zambian may be more "objective" about him than a German or a Jew: but will he understand Hitler better? Even more important than the relative distance or proximity of place is the relative influence of time — by which I do not only mean the "participant" condition of a contemporary or of an eyewitness but something else: the influence of history. Hitler and Hitlerism were an exceptional, but not entirely isolable, episode in the history of Germany and of the German people. Hitler was exceptional, but German nationalism was not. It preceded him; and his popularity among Germans was inconceivable — it would have been impossible — without German nationalism. Of course this is not a uniquely German phenomenon. Thinking and "observation" interfere with the "object," not only because of present mental conditions but also because of the past. It is not only that what happens is inseparable from what people think happens; what people think about their collective or national past is inseparable from their thinking about their present. Their ideas about their history shapes their politics.[10]

That the very act of observing and measuring may alter the physical object is the essence of the Uncertainty or Inde-

10. There are many examples of this: of so many present political and ideological inclinations dependent on thinking back about the Second World War, and not only in Germany. On the one hand the sometimes extreme anxiety and sensitivity of the press and of some people reporting right-wing appearances and manifestations, all due to their ideas and thoughts about World War II; on the other hand the strong inclinations of so-called right-wing and populist parties and people toward "revisionist" interpretations of World War II are fundamental ingredients of their political views of their country and of the world, in many instances.

terminacy principle. This effect is observable in many other phenomena, perhaps especially in mass democratic societies, particularly involving popularity and publicity. There are innumerable examples when the reporting of, or the publicity given to, acts (let alone ideas) stimulates the sudden and multiplying appearance of many similar acts. That impressions of popularity generate choices and acts is nothing new; in its own way it belongs to the history of fashions. But the publicization of popularity is more than an impression: it generates popularity. By repeating and repeating that someone or something or even some idea is popular it may become popular. One lamentable example—and application—thereof is a function of "polls" (often also of news items) and then of their publication, whereby potentialities (the "prediction" of how many people may or will vote) may become actualities.[11]

Many of these exemplifications of a "Heisenberg effect" may be superficial. Yet they tend to confirm the limits of Objectivity and of Objectivism in both the physical and the nonphysical world. In the latter, of course, the applications of Indeterminacy are limited: the very act of observing alters the nature of the object only when its quantum numbers are small. Still this involves, after all, elementary particles of matter. Thus quantum physics does not allow a completely objective descrip-

---

11. This may relate to what, in some of my writings, I have called a mutation in the structure of events. The accumulation of opinions may be more important than the accumulation of capital. The prediction of opinions may create public opinion, just as the prediction of profits may lead to a rise in the price of shares.

tion of nature. To describe "as it really happened" — the famous desideratum of historical description (or, perhaps, more than description: a definition) stated by the great German historian Ranke more than 150 years ago — is an unfulfillable desideratum in the world of matter too. "In our century," Heisenberg wrote in *The Physicist's Conception of Nature,* "it has become clear that the desired objective reality of the elementary particle is too crude an oversimplification of what really happens."[12]

A widespread and lamentable intellectual tendency is the one to nominalism. "Definitions" said Dr. Johnson, "are tricks for pedants" (a maxim wonderfully exemplified by Gradgrind in Dickens's *Hard Times*). To this habit not only scientists but many kinds of political thinkers have been prone. (The categor-

12. "As a final consequence, the natural laws formulated mathematically in quantum theory no longer deal with the elementary particles themselves but with our knowledge of them." In *Physics and Philosophy:* "We cannot completely objectify the result of an observation, we cannot describe what 'happens' between [one] observation and the next. . . . Any statement about what has 'actually happened' is a statement in terms of the classical [Newtonian] concepts and — because of the thermodynamics and of the uncertainty relations — by its very nature incomplete with respect to the details of the atomic events involved. The demand 'to describe what happens' in the quantum-theoretical process between two successive observations is a contradiction *in adjecto.*" In biology, too, "it may be important for a complete understanding that the questions are asked by the species man which itself belongs to the genus of living organisms, in other words, that we already know [I would say: understand] what life is even before we have defined it scientifically."

ical attribution of motives, one of the most lamentable habits of the twentieth century, involves almost always a definition of sorts.) Many historians, who ought to know that the instrument of their craft consists of words, should have been aware that their duty is description, not definition. Often they were not. Here are at least three examples.

One of them is the category of "totalitarian" or "totalitarianism" applied to Hitler.[13] This is mistaken, at least for two reasons. One is that no government, not even the worst kind of tyranny, can be total. (A police state and totalitarianism are *not* the same things.) Also, a feature of Hitler's Third Reich was the continued existence of many traditional German customs and other "free" habits of everyday life (meaning here nothing more than habits not explicitly forbidden by governmental rules and regulations), contributing, alas, to Hitler's popularity. More significant is Hitler's own recognition of the limits of totalitarianism, meaning the total control of the state. He did not use the word "total." He also claimed — alas, with some substance — that he was a democratic ruler *par excellence,* since he was supported by the great majority of the German people. Significant of his revolutionary ideology was his often expressed disdain for the supremacy of the state (in this his philosophy was contrary

13. This habit became near-universal after 1949, after a — much belated — Western, and especially American, realization of the tyranny of Stalin, consequently putting him (and Communism) in the same category as Hitler and National Socialism. This was exemplified by Hannah Arendt's *The Origin of Totalitarianism,* a thoroughly flawed book for very many reasons (including her decision to add two hasty chapters about Communism to her anti-Nazi thesis . . . in 1949–1951).

not only to Hegel's but also to Mussolini's and Stalin's). The state belongs to the past, he said; the *Volk,* the people, came before the state and supersede and survive it. The state is not much more than a rigid and constricting framework, a *"Zwangs-form"*; it is the Volk that matter; and Hitler's state, the Third Reich, is an instrument of the Volk.[14]

This was one of the essential differences between Hitler and Mussolini, who declared: "It is not the people who make the state but the state that makes the people." Campaigning against the individualism of Italians, Mussolini tried to institutionalize and enforce the submission of the individual to the state. He, unlike Hitler, occasionally used "totalitarian" as an adjective (as a matter of fact, it may be Mussolini who invented the word, as early as 1926), even though his Italian regime was authoritarian rather than totalitarian. That is one — but only one — reason why the frequent (and originally Communist-inspired) defini-tion of Hitler and Hitlerism as "Fascist" is wrong. A massive work by the German historian Ernst Nolte in the 1960s, *Three Faces of Fascism,* categorized and defined three right-wing move-

14. Hitler in Munich, November 1934: "In Germany bayonets do not terrorize people. . . . I have not been imposed by anyone upon this people. From this people I have grown up, in the people I have remained, to the people I return. My pride is that I know no statesman in the world who with greater right that I can say that he is representative of the people." Salzburg, April 1938: "In the beginning was the Volk, and only then came the Reich." Nuremberg, 5 September 1934: "Foreigners may say that the state created us. No! We are the State! We follow the orders of no earthly power but those of God who created the German people! On us depends the state!"

ments of the twentieth century: the French Action Française, Mussolini's Italian Fascism, and Hitler's National Socialism. Nolte was wrong: the Action Française had been a pre-Fascist and Hitler and Hitlerism a post-Fascist phenomenon.[15]

But it is not only German historians who have not come to terms with Hitler. The continuing and protracted use (or, rather, misuse) of the "fascist" category has been the outcome of the mental, or perhaps psychic, discomfort of intellectuals having to face the condition that Hitler and National Socialism were a phenomenon to which such categories as "reactionary" or "right-wing" did not properly apply — whence their adoption of the adjective and the categorical definition of Hitler and the Third Reich as "Fascist." To carry this even further: our basic political definitions, originating in France after the French Revolution, "Right" and "Left," in Hitler's case will not do. Was he, for example, to the "Right" or to the "Left" of Churchill? (Or of the Pope?) In his case, none of these definitions will do.[16]

Of course science does depend on categories and definitions. But we know — or ought to know — that definitions have their limitations. For one thing, they consist of and depend on and are expressed by words: and words are necessarily imprecise

15. During the following thirty-five years Nolte, one of the two principal German historians on the "Right" side of the *Historikerstreit*, became an acceptable German historian of "revisionism," writing questionable books praising some of the achievements of the Third Reich.
16. The English wag who, upon the news of the 1939 Hitler-Stalin pact, said that "All the Isms are Wasms" (one of my favorite phrases) was right rather than wrong.

and malleable — which qualifies (and sometimes even adds to) their meaning. We cannot define the unavoidable limits of their applicability. "This is true even of the simplest and most general concepts like 'existence' and 'space and time.' . . . The words 'position' and 'velocity' of an electron, for instance, seemed . . . clearly defined concepts within the mathematical framework of Newtonian mechanics. But actually they were not well defined, as is seen from the relations of Uncertainty. One may say that regarding their position in Newtonian mechanics they were well defined, but in their relation to nature they were not."[17] Here again our recognition of the limitations of definitions in the historical and the scientific universe (or, rather, in our historical and scientific knowledge of the world) coincide and correspond.

I have emphasized Hitler's popularity, which was extraordinary in its nature and in its extent. It was not comparable to the popularity of most other dictators. He often said that he was not a dictator (and there were some reasons for him to make such an assertion); more important, he knew (and we know, or ought to know) that without his popularity he could not have achieved anything. But Hitler's popularity was not a simple matter.

Numbers are insufficient to define or explain it. We pos-

17. Heisenberg, quoted in *Historical Consciousness,* p. 281.

sess a few statistics about the popularity of the Hitler regime. Himmler's secret police took polls during the war; they are, within their limits, telling. But only within limits. If, after careful and successful research, including hitherto unavailable evidence, a historian or a political scientist were to "prove" that, at a certain time, only 20 percent of the German people (or inhabitants of a particular region, or town) were unquestioning adherents of Hitler, this does not mean that 80 percent were his potential (let alone actual) opponents. Conversely, if such a study would "prove" that only 10 percent of Germans were opposed to Hitler and/or to National Socialism, this does not mean that 90 percent were unquestioning adherents. Of course this is applicable to other political phenomena in other places too. But it should be sufficient for us to understand that neither material or electoral or opinion statistics are adequate for the understanding of Hitler's impact on the German people.

There *are* relationships that can be expressed, illustrated, or demonstrated by numbers. But relationships always involve something more than matters of quantity—surely when we think or talk about the relations of human beings. However, we now know that mathematics itself necessarily consists of relationships—whence the *absolute* truthfulness of mathematics has been proved an illusion. At the beginning of the Modern Age, Galileo could say: "The book of nature is written in the language of mathematics," with which his contemporary Descartes wholly agreed. Other seventeenth-century contemporaries: Hobbes: Geometry "is the only science that it hath pleased God hitherto to bestow upon mankind." Spinoza: "If mathematics did not exist, man would not know what truth is." Einstein still thought so, three centuries later. No: if man did not exist, there would be no mathematics. In 1931 the absoluteness of mathematical "truth" was disproved by Gödel's famous theorem, according to which mathematics, too, is dependent on its own preconceptions.[18]

A few years before Gödel physicists began to ask much the same question. Bohr and Heisenberg asked whether it was true that only such experimental formulations of nature can arise as can be expressed through mathematical formalism. Mathematics provides most important and telling formulations of certain material realities; but mathematics does not preempt those realities completely or indefinitely. Quantum physics also found that certain mathematical statements depend on the sequential time element in their measurement: that P times Q is not always the equivalent of Q times P when, for example, P means momentum and Q position.[19] In other words: the order in which certain mathematical (and physical) operations are performed may affect their results; they are not independent of human concepts of time and perhaps even of purpose.

18. A century before Gödel, Goethe: "What is exact in mathematics except its own exactitude?"
19. It may be needless to argue that this is applicable to human or historic conditions, and not only to measurements of "popularity." One admittedly crude example: In 1940 Germany's victory over France was not equivalent to France's defeat, either in its effects or in its significance. The latter was greater, and more enduring. Why? because history, and life, move forward, whereas mathematics is necessarily static. We perceive the relative "greatness," the "size" of events, from their consequences.

This is one reason to prefer the term "event" to "fact," in history as well as in physics.

I have now written enough about the inevitable relationship of the knower with the known, involving participation. But there is of course another kind of inevitable relationship, inherent also in the recognition that we perceive (let alone understand) "facts" through their associations. In Hitler's case both our interest in and our judgment of him are not only dependent on but generated by our comparison of Hitler and of the Third Reich with other modern "totalitarian" dictatorships (though as we have seen above, these terms may be questionable: in at least some ways the Third Reich was less than "totalitarian," and Hitler was both more and less than a dictator).

We have seen that an increasing number of "conservative" historians, as well as other writers, especially in Germany and Austria but also elsewhere, have produced works comparing Hitler with Stalin, and the evils of National Socialism with the evils of Communism. They compare statistics of their victims and the extents of their crimes — with the purpose, in almost every case, of qualifying and reducing, at least implicitly, the uniqueness of the evidence of the evil record of National Socialism and of course of Hitler. Indeed, some of these historians have gone beyond *comparing*. They *relate* Stalin to Hitler, and Communism to National Socialism, by arguing the priority of the former: that Hitler and National Socialism were an expectable, and probably inevitable, reaction to the crimes committed by Lenin and Stalin and Communism.[20] This is not the place to argue or to illustrate that what Hitler and National Socialism and many of the German people (among the most educated peoples in the world) wrought in the center of Europe was something else and something more ominous than what Stalin (and, before him, Lenin) had brought about in a backward country. And while history does not repeat itself, many of Stalin's deeds (and his reasoning) were at least comparable to those of Ivan the Terrible, while the uniqueness of Hitler should be apparent, too, from the condition that he was (and is) not comparable to any German leader in the past.

But there is another consideration of the relationship of Hitler's effects that has, by and large, not received the attention it may deserve. This is that the influence of Hitler (and National Socialism) on the development of Stalin's mind (and of Russian Communism) and on the development of Mussolini's mind (and of Italian Fascism) was much more than any of the reverse influences. Yes, Mussolini and Stalin preceded the rule of Hitler, and both of them had some influence on Hitler himself; but when we consider the historical development of the three dic-

---

20. One of their, regrettably accumulating, arguments is their employment of "evidence" that Hitler's invasion of Russia in 1941 was a reaction to Stalin's plans to attack Germany in 1941. Not only is this untrue but the very opposite is what had happened then: not because Stalin was anything like a pacifist but because at the time he had acted like a coward. He tried in every way to convince Hitler that he wanted to maintain (indeed, to intensify) their good relations, even at the cost of forbidding serious Russian defense measures up to the last minute, withholding any Russian response to German provocations, even in view of the massive evidence of vast German forces gathering across the frontier and preparing to attack.

tatorships, and of their ideas, Hitler and National Socialism had an increasing and evident influence and impact on the other two. I wrote before that it is an egregious error to define Hitler as a "Fascist"; it would be even more nonsensical to apply the adjective "Communist" to either Mussolini or to Hitler. But National Socialism, nationalist socialism, was applicable both to Mussolini and Stalin, especially as time went on. For all kinds of reasons, and in different circumstances, both Mussolini and Stalin became increasingly anti-Semitic and more and more nationalist — this is especially noteworthy in Stalin's case. This phenomenon illustrates many things: the strength and the attraction of National Socialism; the impact of Hitler and of his many successes; and — in addition to the historical forces of the 1930s and early 1940s — the universal human tendency of people to adjust their ideas to circumstances, rather than adjusting circumstances to their ideas (the latter being much more rare and much less successful than the former). The character of men as well as of nations and movements is most apparent — and judgeable — from their relations and effects on other men and nations and movements. In sum, relationships (and their perception) are *more than secondary elements* of the development, indeed, of the essence of events.

Much of this we now know, too, when it comes to physical "facts" (or, rather, as I wrote before: *events*). Modern physics now admits that important factors may not have clear and precise definitions; on the other hand, these factors *may* be clearly defined with regard to their connections. These relationships are thus not of secondary but of primary importance. Just as no "fact" can stand alone, apart from its associations with other "facts," modern physics now tends to divide the world not so much into different groups of objects as into different groups of connections. In mathematics, too, it is being increasingly recognized that the functions of connections may be more important than the static definitions of "factors." Euclid said that a point is something which has no parts and which occupies no space. At the height of positivism, and during the last phase of unquestionable classical physics — say, around 1890 — it was generally believed that an even more perfect statement would consist in exact definitions of "parts" and of "space." But mathematicians as well as physicists have since learned that this tinkering with definitions tends to degenerate into a useless semantic nominalism. Consequently they no longer bother to find absolute definitions of "points" and "lines." Their interest is directed, instead, to the axiom that two points can always be connected by a line — thus to the relationships of lines and points and connections.

History does not repeat itself, scientific experiments must be repeatable; history is unpredictable, science must not be; uniqueness marks human existence, science must depend on regularity. Much is true in these juxtapositions, but not entirely — or no longer so. In history we can, though only within limits, at least predict what is not likely to happen, rather than what is likely to happen. This, in other words, means potentiality, rather than actuality; or, more exactly, potentiality within actuality and also the reverse. That potentiality, or probability, now involves scientific knowledge too is something to which I must turn at the end of this subchapter; but before that I must again illustrate the existence of unpredictability with the example of Hitler.

Unpredictable: unlikely. The two terms are not the same; but both involve mental functions, probable or improbable anticipations of expectations. This does not deny Kierkegaard's wise formula ("We live forward but we can only think backward"), because our thinking of possibilities — looking forward — is inevitably dependent on circumstances, indeed on our knowledge and/or understanding of the past. Well, the entire Hitler phenomenon, producing and influencing much of the history of the twentieth century (and not only in Germany and Europe), meaning the appearance of a dynamic and powerful nationalism, a Third Force between Communism and Capitalism, or Russia and America, etc., etc., was rather unpredictable; and even more unpredictable was the possibility of an obscure and lonely and classless and foreign-born demagogue becoming the chancellor of Germany, assisted by the conservative establishment of the German nation. Yet this happened, for at least two major reasons. One was the operation of Hitler's free will, that Hitler *wanted* it to happen; what men want to be is often even more important than what they "are"; like Alexander or Bonaparte or Stalin, Hitler was not a native-born leader, but he believed that it was his task (and destiny) to become the leader of the German people. The other, allied, reason was his recognition of the potential (rather than actual) appeal of the ideas he represented and, even more, expressed. Still: was Hitler's rise to power predictable, or likely? Before 1932 it was not; but *he* surely believed that it was. Nor was it inevitable that he and his Germany would lose the war: in 1940 and 1941 he came close to winning it.

However: my argument is not an emphasis on the will to power. The other, and perhaps more interesting, problem or question is this: were Hitler's actions predictable? Many people, including historians, think so even now. They rely—not without some reason—on *Mein Kampf,* Hitler's own proposition of his ideological world-view, including his concrete propositions about Russia, France, England, Italy, Jews, which he then seems to have accordingly and rigidly and ideologically followed and put into practice throughout his stunning career. But this is too simple. Apart from the—not infrequent—instances in which Hitler himself said that *Mein Kampf* ought not to be taken verbatim or even too seriously, the claim that because of *Mein Kampf* many of Hitler's choices of actions were predictable is an imprecise exaggeration—as is the, alas, still widespread argument that the Depression, the German economic crisis in 1930–1932, made Hitler's rise to power not only likely but unavoidable. Again, apart from the fact that Hitler had virtually no economic program in 1930–1932 (which, at least to my mind, was an advantage, not a handicap), depression and unemployment in Germany led to a Hitler, while depression and unemployment in the United States led to a Roosevelt. Adolf Hitler, despite his often repetitious and dogmatic declarations, was not predictable. Despite all of his anti-Communist ideology in 1939, he made a pact with Stalin. Then in 1941 he invaded Russia—not simply because of the principles of anti-Communism or of "Lebensraum," proposed in detail in *Mein Kampf;* but mainly because, not unlike Napoleon, he convinced himself that an independent or neutral Russia was England's last hope on the Continent. There are parallels between Napoleon and Hitler, the first a Corsican-born Frenchman, the second an Austrian-born German, and both starting their invasion of Russia almost on the same day of the year; still, they were very different human beings.[21] And the same Hitler who declared and preached and objurgated about race and Jews throughout his career would say often during the late 1930s and early 1940s that race was a "myth," and (in 1945) that Jews, too, are not a physical but a "spiritual" race. Like the life of every other human being, Hitler's life was marked by unpredictableness; his mind took unlikely turns on occasion.

Hitler's life demonstrates the exceptional potentialities of willpower; but the human capacity (and divine gift) of free will is *not* why unpredictability must be recognized as valid throughout the world, *including* our very knowledge of physical matter. It must be recognized mainly because of the limits of mechanical causality. We have seen that the direct and mechanical attribution of causes to effects is unhistorical and unreal. This has now become demonstrable in the very world of physics. Uncertainty figures among the "causes" of every subatomic event. More concretely: the temperature of an atom is not an actuality but only a "potentia." An accurate description of an elementary particle is impossible — on one level because of the dependence

21. Also: Napoleon, who actually occupied Moscow for a few weeks, was defeated by the Russian winter, whereas Hitler, whose army could not reach Moscow, survived the cruel Russian winter; as he said in April 1942: "We have mastered a destiny which broke another man 130 years ago."

of every description on words. But that is not all: a particle "exists" (meaning: it can be observed) only as a probability function, that is, as a possibility or a tendency for being. And this probability is not merely the addition of the element of "chance"; it is also something different from mathematical formulations of probabilities. Probability is never definable as a particular event at a particular moment. According to Heisenberg, "It represents a tendency of events and our knowledge of events."[22]

"Quantification" became a fad within the historical profession, gaining respectability in the 1960s. This is not the place to describe why and how many of its applications are insufficient, and even misleading — except perhaps to say that while the very purpose of historical "quantification" is, or claims to be, to establish "facts" that are verifiable, the principal problem of the historical statistics quantification employs resides in their often very questionable verifiability.

The history of Hitler illustrates how even verifiable statistics may be insufficient. Statistics cannot explain the extraordi-

22. Also Louis Victor de Broglie in 1939: "The notions of causality and of individuality have had to undergo a fresh scrutiny, and it seems certain that this major crisis, affecting the guiding principles of our physical concepts will be the source of philosophical consequences which cannot be yet clearly perceived." Twenty years later this historian was attempting to recognize some of them; and another forty years later — at the very end of the Modern Age — this book represents a, necessarily, imperfect, attempt to summarize their meaning.

nary achievements of the economy and the productive capacity
of the Third Reich, the swift rise of German national prosperity
soon after 1933, the astonishing quantity and quality of their
armaments thereafter, and the no less extraordinary prevalence
and functioning of the industrial production and of the food
available to the German people till the very end, even when
thousands of tons of bombs were raining on their cities and
towns. Armed as they were with statistics (and not often inexact
ones) throughout the war, the economic experts of the Allies
were stunned by this condition. Yet the religious thinker Simone Weil understood this phenomenon at once. During the
war, in 1942, she wrote: "If Hitler despises economy, it is probably not simply because he understands nothing about it. It is
because he *knows* (it is one of the notions of simple common
sense that he clearly possesses and that can be called inspired
since such ideas are so little understood) that economy is not an
independent reality and as a result does not really have laws. . . .
It seems to me difficult to deny that Hitler conceives, and conceives clearly . . . a kind of physics of human matter. . . . He
possesses an exact notion of the power of force."[23]

Hitler's extraordinary power, his extraordinary rise, his extraordinary successes, his extraordinary appeal to his people

23. I have quoted this often. Also the excellent German historical essayist
Sebastian Haffner: "Was the German economic miracle [and it was a
miracle] of the Thirties really Hitler's achievement? In spite of all conceiv-
able objections one will probably have to reply in the affirmative. It is
entirely true that . . . economic matters, prior to 1933, had played virtually
no part in his political thinking." *The Meaning of Hitler*, New York, 1979,
pp. 28–29.

were largely due to his conviction of the primacy of mind over matter. There is, at first sight, a paradox here. His character, and his self-discipline, were strong. Yet the fundamental source of his strength was hatred. Compared to the power of his hatred, even his love of the German people — the living purpose of a national leader — amounted to less. In this he was quite unlike Napoleon. Even though hatred often results in physical inclinations and physical acts, it is essentially a matter of mind. And while hatred amounts to a moral weakness,[24] it can be, alas, often, and at least in the short run, a source of strength.

Hitler's people — including many of his National Socialist leaders, and most of his generals — did not really share such hatreds. They were, instead, inspired by a kind of confidence, national and ideological, that led to their contempt for their adversaries, opponents, enemies, victims — whence their brutalities. That confidence was the main source of the extraordinary successes and achievements of the Third Reich, including a world war during which fewer than eighty million Germans prevailed over the continent of Europe and fought for nearly six years, against the overwhelming power of hundreds of millions of their enemies who could not conquer them until the very end. No material or statistical explanation for this will do. Nor is there any material explanation for Hitler's popularity among his people before the war. Soon after he had become Chancel-

---

24. Franz Stangl, the commander of the Treblinka death camp, said after the war to a journalist who asked him before his execution: "Do you think that that time in Poland taught you anything?" Stangl: "Yes. That everything human has its origins in human weakness."

lor, the startling economic improvement and the sudden evap-
oration of unemployment were consequences as well as causes
of his popularity.

Still: extraordinary as Hitler's career was, he and his Germany *were* eventually conquered by the material (and numeri-
cal) superiority of their opponents. (That, too, was not merely
a question of matter; it was inseparable from the conviction of
their otherwise very disparate leaders and of their peoples that
they must extirpate Hitler and conquer the Third Reich entirely.) We must understand that the frequent primacy of mind
over matter does *not* mean their separation; rather, the contrary.
It is not only that Christians (and idealists) must understand
what many of the greatest and most ascetic Christian saints and
Christian thinkers have asserted: that we must be grateful to
God not only for having created us with our minds, but for
having created matter, because matter in itself is good. (Yes, *all*
matter; it is only human interference and participation that can
render it poisonous or evil.) What belongs here is the necessary
understanding that, three or more centuries after Descartes and
Galileo and Newton, the inseparability of matter and mind has
been demonstrated — and ought so to be recognized — by physics. Matter is transmutable: the formerly categorical distinctions
between animate and inanimate, between organic and inorganic
matter are no longer absolute, just as the partition of the world
into objects and subjects no longer holds, and just as in physics
the object of research is no longer nature itself but our investigation of nature. This does not mean that physical events *depend*
on our observations. It means that our cognition of their exis-

tence, rather than our "observation," is an inevitable element;[25] that the science of matter deals not "only" with matter but with the knowledge of matter as man thinks and describes it. The scientific method must be conscious of its own, human limitations. The materialist view of the world is both insufficient and misleading, because it fails to take into account the inevitable intrusion of the mind.

The very recognition of this has been a historical development:

> The mechanics of Newton and all the other parts of classical physics constructed after its model started out from the assumption [I would say; tacitly accepted as an assumption] that one can describe the world without speaking about God or ourselves. This possibility seemed almost a necessary condition for natural science in general.
>
> But at this point this situation changed to some extent through quantum physics. . . . We cannot disregard the fact [I would say: condition] that science is formed by men. Natural science does not simply describe and explain nature; it is a part of this interplay between nature and ourselves; it describes nature as exposed to our method of questioning. This was a possibility of

25. Goethe: "The term 'observation' is in some ways too passive."

which Descartes could not have thought [?]²⁶
but it makes the sharp separation between the
world and the I impossible.

If one follows the great difficulty which even
eminent scientists like Einstein had in understanding and accepting the Copenhagen interpretation of quantum theory, one can trace the
roots of this difficulty to the Cartesian partition.
This partition has penetrated deeply into the human [I would say Western] mind during the
three centuries following Descartes and it will
take a long time for it to be replaced by a really
different attitude toward the problem of reality.²⁷
[See Correspondences, pp. 186–187.]

There is another paradox latent in the example of Hitler.
His mind gave him confidence, and successes; but his mind also
contributed, and caused, his downfall. There is one particular,
and paradoxical, example of this. He believed — against almost
all evidences — in 1938 (which was his triumphant year) that he
would not live long (he was less than fifty then); and that consequently he had to speed up the timetable of Germany's con-
quests. He convinced himself — wrongly — that time (because

26. Why not? Pascal did. Cassirer: "There is in the Cartesian mind a kind
of distrust, almost an antipathy, to history."
27. Heisenberg, quoted in *Historical Consciousness,* p. 286.

of the Western powers' rearmament) was working against him *and* against his Germany, which was not at all the case. Beginning in 1938, he thought that he was actually more ill than he was. Yet "actually," in this context, is an imprecise word. His increasingly frequent gastrointestinal ailments were, to use a modern and not very satisfactory word, at least to some extent "psychosomatic." Their etiology, as indeed is the etiology of many such ailments, was existential, not merely physical — and this was bound to be an exaggerated condition in the life of a man whose force of character had its source in his belief in the power of the mind and of the will.

Perhaps we may detect God's hand in the development of this paradoxical condition: this man, who so often spoke of (and exemplified) the primacy of mind over matter, and of spirit over flesh, now started to move downhill and eventually into catastrophe — because of the developing state of his mind, which affected his body, whose symptoms, in turn, impressed him with the deep inner sense that he had not long to live. His belief in mind over matter raised him to the highest power on a continent; and this belief was to destroy him in the end.

However, more important and more telling, and, for our purposes, more evident than the etiology of Hitler's illnesses is the failure of his idealism. He was a deterministic idealist. He thought that the power of the spirit of German National Socialism was sufficient unto itself to defy much of the world, including the material power of his enemies. He was not alone in this. There were two of his best generals, Alfred Jodl (on 7 November 1943): "We will win because we must win, for otherwise world history will have lost its meaning." And Field Marshal

Walther Model on 29 March 1945 (note the date!): "In our struggle for the ideals of National Socialism . . . it is a mathematical certainty [!] that we will win, as long as our beliefs and will remain unbroken." Determinism, whether materialist or idealist, whether mechanical or spiritual, is always wrong.

And in this respect Hitler was not an isolated phenomenon. After 1870 in Europe there appeared a philosophical and ideological reaction against the materialistic and positivistic thinking of the nineteenth century. The main proponents and representatives of this reaction were German. It included a reaction against the French Enlightenment and also against the French Revolution of 1789. This antimaterialist reaction in Europe, from about 1875 to 1941 — more accurately, this post-materialist and, yes, post-modern movement in European intellectual history — cannot be properly assayed without considering the history of nations at the same time. In 1871 Ernest Renan said to the French that the victory of the Germans at Sedan had been the victory of the German schoolmaster. In 1945 the defeat of the Third Reich was largely a defeat of German extreme idealism — more precisely: of idealistic German national fanaticism. It is true that, as Péguy said, the intrusion of politics and of its rhetoric leads to the degeneration of truth and of thought. But it is precisely because of this pervasiveness of political power that the history of ideas cannot be treated as a specific and isolated "field." We have seen that scientists, too, are not at all immune to the prevailing political and philosophical ideas of their times. A philosophical skepticism of causality, part and parcel of their reaction against the rationalism of the French Enlightenment, existed among German thinkers in the early 1920s. It preceded Heisenberg's own discovery of the limits of mechanical causality. This does not mean that Heisenberg's discovery (not to speak of its experimental evidences) was a predictable result of a "Zeitgeist." Our ideas are the results of our choices. Yes, our choices are influenced (and sometimes even produced) by our times and by the world around us; but the consequences of our ideas, what we do with our ideas, are not simple results. Ideas do have consequences, but these are seldom direct or simple or unequivocal: the intrusion of minds, and of human inclinations, occurs; ideas and their consequences are formed by their wearers and carriers themselves.

There is, moreover, a duality in every human being, including Hitler. He believed in the fundamental and categorical importance of race; yet he often denied racial theories and categories. He declared the superior importance of people and of their beliefs to the state; yet many of his political and strategic decisions were made on the basis of statecraft, not on ideological preferences, let alone racial or national sympathies. He excoriated materialistic views of history; yet he was attracted by supermodern projects of technology, of travel, including travel into space. Finally, moved as he was by fanatical hatreds, we can also detect in Hitler, here and there, elements of fear.

In this respect a last word about National Socialism — and about the dangers of a deterministic idealism. The failure of materialism, and of the bourgeois standards of an age, opened up a spiritual and intellectual vacuum which after 1930, and also in our times, was due to be filled somehow. The unpredictable and surprising rise of National Socialism, its attraction, including its attraction to some very intelligent people between the two world wars, was due not only to the dislike or even fear of Communism, but also to the disillusionment with the material- ism of the international capitalist order (or disorder), and with what seemed to be an antiquated and hypocritical and corrupt liberal parliamentary order (or disorder). National Socialism was a new third force, youthful and vital, the opposite of any- thing "reactionary," attractive to many young people. Sixty or seventy years later, in spite of the accumulated evidence of Hit- ler's brutalities, such inclinations continue to exist. Interna- tional Communism is gone; but there are few reasons to believe that the post-capitalist and post-bourgeois materialism of an American type inspires or will continue to inspire many young people throughout the world. Once more a new kind of ideol- ogy may fill what is unquestionably a spiritual and intellectual vacuum. The rise in the historical interest in and occasional attraction of National Socialism and of Fascism is but a minor symptom of this. Whether here and there, a reemergence of nationalist socialism (though not in its most brutal Hitlerian form) might fill an ideological vacuum I cannot tell. But the appetite exists: and it exists, often, alas, not only in many kinds of national hatreds but in all kinds of unrestricted spiritualisms, beliefs in mythical faiths, involving more and more beliefs in the existence of supernatural and superterrestrial phenomena (per- haps especially in the Western Hemisphere). We must not (can- not) regret the slow but inexorable decay of a categorical ratio- nalism and of materialism; but aware we must be of the grave dangers and sickening irrational appearances of idealistic deter- minisms of many kinds.

In any event — due to the evolution of consciousness (which

is probably the *only* evolution there is, the Darwinian theory of "evolution" being part of it, and not the converse) the intrusion of mind into matter increases. In other words, we are facing the gradual spiritualization of matter;[28] many of the results of which are still unpredictable and even unimaginable, good or bad as they may be — but surely bad when and if the spiritualization of matter devolves into a false idealism.

28. One evident example already among us: what happened to money. A century ago, in 1900, money was physically solid, and its paper certificates exchangeable to gold or silver at par value. Yet for decades now, our money or stocks and bonds are not even on paper or in our *actual* possession; they are *potential* "values," consisting of configurations of graphic dust recorded on disks or films, in distant institutions somewhere else. This is explained to us as part and parcel of the Information Revolution. Yet the very word "information" is false: it is *not in-formation;* it *does not form* our inner selves. Its proper description is *the imaging of matter.*

Correspondences

The limits of historical knowledge.	We will never know exactly why Hitler became the ruler of Germany.	The limits of scientific certitude.	Impossible to determine the position and the speed of the particle in the same instant.
The limits of historical objectivity.	German nationalists were not only products of history: their writings made history.	The limits of scientific objectivity.	The very act of observing may alter the physical object.
The limits of definitions.	By employing "Fascist" or "right-wing" categories we will not understand Hitler.	The illusory character of nominalism.	The relativity of scientific categories and measurements.
"Facts" do not exist by themselves.	Electoral or opinion-statistics are not adequate for the understanding of Hitler's impact on Germany and its people.	The illusory character of the absolute truth of mathematics.	In subatomic situations $P \times Q$ is not always equivalent to $Q \times P$.
History involves the study of the relationships of men, of nations, of classes, of movements.	Hitler and National Socialism influenced the course of Stalin and Communism and of Mussolini and Fascism more than any of the reverse combinations.	Not the "essence" of "factors" but their relationship matters.	Modern physics proceeds best by examining not different objects but different groups of connections.

Correspondences

Historical thinking is anti-determinist and teleological.	Hitler's potentiality (what he wanted to or could become) was not what he was (in actuality).	The primary importance of potentialities, of tendencies.	The temperature of an atom is only a "potentia."
Historical causality is not mechanical, mostly because of free will. Also: what happens is not separable from what people think happens.	Hitler's choices were often unpredictable.	The limits of mechanical causality.	Matter is transmutable; the sharp distinction between organic and inorganic matter no longer exists.
Historical thinking consists of words.	The evils of Hitler's rule were both causes of and results of his language.	The principles of "classical" physical logic are no longer unconditional.	Physics cannot escape the reality (and the limitations) of language.
The need for a new, historical philosophy.	Men are potentially both beasts and angels; and the sins of the spirit are worse than the sins of the flesh.	At the end of the Modern Age Descartes's partition falls away.	Indeterminacy means the collapse of the division of the world into Objects and Subjects.

FIVE

At the Center of the Universe

✦

"Christians should be the salt, not the
syrup, of the earth."
Bernanos.

Timeliness, and limitations of my
argument. • Heisenberg and Duhem. • At the
center of the universe. • Conditions of
belief. • A necessity for Christians.

Everything has its history, including history. Every
argument, every law, every thesis, every hypothesis
has its history—which means that they cannot be
perfect or complete or eternally unchanging. Of
course this involves the priority of historical over "scientific"
thinking. And that recognitions of the limits of both kinds of
thinking correspond to such an extent that, after more than four
hundred years, the time has come to realize that there is only
one kind of knowledge, dependent on the inevitable limitations
of the human knower. This recognition comes at the end of the
Modern Age, the two great achievements of which were the
invention and the applications of the scientific method and the
evolution of a historical consciousness. Of these great developments the first, naturally and as a matter of course (its development having been inseparable from the modern idea of Progress), has been widely recognized and appreciated, while the
second has not. Yet since the second amounts to nothing less

than a knowledge of human beings about themselves, there are ample reasons to appreciate, widen, and elevate its importance, especially at the end of the twentieth century, during which we have had plenty of shocking evidences of the complexities and dualities of human beings, including their capacity for evil. (Whence probably the rising appetite for history, at a time of general decay of civilization. Still, this may be an ephemeral, though not insignificant, phenomenon.) Cartesian and Newtonian science led to the fabulous capacity of mankind to manage *things*. But we ought to recognize that not only the fundament of the above but its *prior* necessity is our understanding of human beings — and of their place in the universe, to which this chapter will be addressed.

There exists an extremely important timeliness for this kind of thinking. For the first time since Genesis (or: in the history of mankind) it has now become not only imaginable but possible for human beings to destroy large portions (or, potentially, all) of humanity, and perhaps even most of life on this earth. This may happen by man-made explosions or by man-made poisoning of the atmosphere by disastrous genetic manipulations: we (still fortunately) do not know. But we must take a step back and look and think: this is something new. Need one argue that this new and awful potentiality of mankind's self-destruction elevates the importance of mankind's self-knowledge even above that of its material applications of theoretical "science"?

Still — I am aware of the unavoidable limitations due to the very historicity of my propositions. It may not be likely, but it is not entirely impossible that new discoveries may considerably, or even dramatically, affect the proposition of the all-encompassing nature of historical — that is, human — knowledge. It is also possible that I may have put too much emphasis on the epistemological meaning of quantum theory (which is, after all, a theory), a caveat to which I shall turn in a page or so, in a subchapter about Werner Heisenberg and the French physicist and historian of science Pierre Duhem. But before that I am compelled to admit another evident and common-sense consideration. Whatever quantum theory (and some of its man-made measurements) tells us about the structures and mechanics of subatomic matter, in our everyday world the rapidly increasing applications of physical science and technology still depend on Newtonian physics, no matter how questionable the universal validity of the latter has become. This is especially applicable to computers and also to physical biology. And this condition corresponds to the history, indeed to the retrospect, of the Modern Age. I wrote earlier that the Modern, or the Bourgeois, or the European Age, has hitherto been the richest half-millennium in the history of mankind, in many ways comparable to the classic achievements of the near-millennium of Greece and Rome. And — something that has *not* happened after the end of a previous great epoch — a respect and nostalgia for the achievements of the past five hundred years has begun to emerge. And among its many achievements Newtonian physics will continue to prevail, because of its ever-extending technical applications. And who knows whether (and when) both Newtonian and quantum physics may not be superseded by something else?

Still: my main interest, and the theme of this book, deals not with the applications of physical or of historical theories but with their meaning—in sum, with recognitions of the conditions of human thinking at the end of an age. And because of this I must once more, for the last time, return to Heisenberg and to a fine twentieth-century thinker who preceded him, the French Pierre Duhem.

I need not reiterate my appreciation of Werner Heisenberg. There remain, however, two considerations. One is that Heisenberg's ideas were not uninfluenced by his times: we have seen that there was a chronological, indeed a historical, correspondence between German ideological anti-materialism and anti-mechanical causality after World War I and the germination of Heisenberg's Indeterminism. After his discovery of subatomic Uncertainty, thirty years, including World War II, had to pass until in 1954–1955 Heisenberg's convictions about the philosophical or metaphysical or epistemological consequences of the latter had crystallized. I, for one, am inclined to think that Heisenberg's epistemological propositions may have been an achievement as considerable as his experimental discovery of Uncertainty/Indeterminacy in subatomic physics. Yet convictions are not always final. Heisenberg was to live for another twenty years, during which we saw that he—not quite like, but also not entirely unlike other physicists—was working on an eventual mathematical formulation about the dynamics of

atomic particles.[1] The other consideration is metaphysical. Heisenberg's experimental proofs of his Uncertainty principle established the impossibility of the complete accuracy of the measurement of small particles of matter; but does this impossibility
amount to a limitation of our knowledge of their very existence?
I think so: because of my belief that the existence of anything is
meaningless for us without our knowledge of it, no matter how
imprecise or faint;[2] but this may be one (albeit only one, and a
minor) reason why so few, if any, physicists have paid any attention to Heisenberg's metaphysical propositions during the past
fifty years.

And it is because of metaphysics — and cosmology — that I
must turn briefly to Pierre Duhem. This extraordinary physicist
and philosopher, born in 1861, died in 1916, already broken in

1. Wasn't this an attempt toward another kind of "finality," in addition (or,
perhaps, at least to a limited degree, contrary) to the conclusive character
of his earlier convictions? I dared to ask this in a letter to Heisenberg in
1967. His detailed two-page answer denying this is in my possession.

2. The learned, sometimes brilliant, but interminably opinionated Stan-
ley L. Jaki (one of whose merits is his exegesis of Pierre Duhem) elevates
Einstein and dismisses Heisenberg repeatedly, including this passage in
Jaki's otherwise excellent introduction to *The Physicist as Artist: The Landscapes of Pierre Duhem,* Edinburgh, 1988, p. 2: "The illogical character of
casting Einstein's relativity theory into the moulds of positivism . . . [But
wasn't Einstein a determinist?] . . . Utter disregard for logic has become
part and parcel of the standard [?] philosophical interpretation of quantum mechanics which, as is well known, has Heisenberg's uncertainty
principle as its integral part. Although that principle merely sets a limit to
accuracy in measurement, its standard interpretation . . . is a fallacious
identification of the operationally exact with the ontologically exact." But
isn't experimental science dependent on accuracy?

health, and well before Heisenberg's Indeterminacy/Uncertainty. (I have found no evidence about Einstein appearing in Duhem's writings.) Duhem's greatest contributions were those in the history and in the theory of physics. He *was* a first-class physicist, especially in his work on thermodynamics. Resistance to his appointment to the highest positions of French science was a result of academic politics, connected with Duhem's solitary and, at that time, unusual avowal of his Catholic and conservative beliefs. Yet since his untimely death Duhem's reputation (especially in France but also among many scientists throughout the world) has risen much higher. The astonishing quantity of his writings is startling enough. He wrote (in his careful handwriting) a ten-volume history of physics and cosmology: *Système du monde: Histoire des doctrines cosmologiques de Platon à Copernic,* Paris, 1913–1959 — which, again because of academic and publishing politics, was published only gradually, much of it after his death. While he was working on those volumes he wrote *La Théorie physique: Son objet, sa structure,* first published in 1906, which is more telling for our purposes, and of which an American edition exists: *The Aim and Structure of Physical Theory,* Princeton, 1954, equipped by a detailed foreword by the great French physicist Louis de Broglie, and translated and prefaced by the American physicist Philip P. Wiener.[3]

---

3. This is not the place to list the extraordinary extent of Duhem's works, some of which are now available in English: for example, *To Save the Phenomena: An Essay on the Idea of Physical Theory from Plato to Galileo,* Chicago, 1969 (introduced by Jaki). The very title of the work (Duhem gave it in Greek) corresponds, rather extraordinarily, with Owen Barfield's *Saving the Appearances,* London, 1957 (an American paperback also

What is Duhem's great and lasting achievement? There is — as suggested by the title of his monumental ten-volume work — his historical approach to science: "The history of science alone can keep the physicist from descending into grave errors" (p. 270). Among other things, Duhem established something that was ignored or denied not only by scientists but by nearly all historians: he drew attention to the medieval origins of classical physics, preceding Copernicus, Galileo, Newton. But more

---

exists), including a reference to Duhem ("whose monumental work . . . combines German thoroughness with French lucidity"). *To Save the Phenomena* and *Saving the Appearances* correspond, too, in their emphasis on the inescapable and basic reality of what we see: for Duhem, for example, the sun rising in the east and setting in the west; for Barfield, the existence of a rainbow which is something else than an optical illusion.

To this I must add another stunning achievement of this charming genius (a rare combination!): Duhem's artwork. He was a drawer and a painter of extraordinary ability and beauty. It is the abiding merit of Jaki to have found and collected most of Duhem's drawings and paintings in a beautifully produced album: *The Physicist as Artist: The Landscapes of Pierre Duhem*, Edinburgh, 1988, with an erudite introduction.

Again a correspondence. There are many physicists who have been addicted to music (and there are correspondences between the structures of cosmological and musical harmonies); but few physicists whose inspiration was artistic and visual. And it was a visual recognition that inspired Heisenberg at a decisive moment. He told us that at the age of sixteen he had read in a Gymnasium physics textbook that atoms were the smallest indivisible building stones of matter: but the illustration in the text showed atoms connected with hooks and eyes which were supposed to represent their chemical bonds. "I was greatly put off by this illustration. I was enraged that such idiotic things should be presented in a textbook of physics. I thought that if atoms were indeed such structures as this book made out — if their structure was complicated enough for them to have hooks and eyes — then they could not possibly be the smallest indivisible building stones of matter."

important for our purposes is Duhem's clear and severe exposition of the inescapably theoretical essence of physics. Let me illustrate this merely by a few titles of his successive subchapters:

> Theory anticipating experiment.
>
> The mathematics of approximation.
>
> An experiment in physics is not simply the observation of a phenomenon; it is, besides, the theoretical interpretation of the phenomenon.
>
> The result of an experiment in physics is an abstract and symbolic judgment.
>
> The laws of physics are symbolic relations.
>
> A law of physics is, properly speaking, neither true nor false but approximate.
>
> Every law of physics is provisional and relative because it is approximate.
>
> Every physical law is provisional because it is symbolic.
>
> Hypotheses are not the product of sudden creation, but the result of progressive evolution.
>
> The importance in physics of the historical method.

"The Physicist Does Not Choose the Hypotheses in Which He Will Base a Theory; They Germinate in Him Without Him" (title of subchapter 3, in part II, chapter VII). Duhem begins: "The evolution which produced the system of universal gravity slowly unfolded itself in the course of centuries; thus we have been able to follow step by step the process through which the idea gradually rose to the degree of perfection given it by Newton." This process is, more than often, slow. "A hundred and forty years separate Copernicus' main work from Newton's." At times it is rapid: in 1819–1823 less than four years separated the publication of Oersted's electromagnetic experiment from Ampère's conclusive paper presented at the Paris Académie des Sciences.

Duhem makes a brilliant distinction between accuracy and precision/certainty:

> A law of physics possesses a certainty much less immediate and much more difficult to estimate than a law of common sense, but it surpasses the latter by the minute and detailed precision of its predictions.
>
> Take the common-sense law: "In Paris the sun rises every day in the east, climbs the sky, then comes down and sets in the west" and compare it with the formulas telling us the coordinates of the sun's center at each instant within about a second. . . . The laws of physics can acquire this minuteness of detail only by sacrificing something of the fixed and absolute certainty of common-sense laws. There is a sort of balance between precision and certainty; one cannot be increased except to the detriment of the other.[4]

4. Was this a forerunner — or another version — of Heisenberg's discovery about electrons? Precision > < certainty: Velocity > < position?

> The miner who presents me with a stone can tell
> me without hesitation or qualification that it
> contains gold; but the chemist who shows me a
> shiny ingot, telling me, "It is pure gold," has to
> add the qualification "or nearly pure"; he cannot
> affirm that the ingot does not retain minute
> traces of impurities.
>
> A man may swear to tell the truth, but it is
> not in his power to tell the whole truth and
> nothing but the truth.[5]

The no less startling appendix to *The Aim and Structure of Physical Theory* is entitled "Physics of a Believer." Here again Duhem proceeds historically, giving one example of his own personal history. His theory of thermodynamics, he writes, was the result of an intuition which was due to his recognition of the impossibility of proving it by experiment. Answering some of his students' questions:

> We then had an intuition of the truths which
> since that time we have continually affirmed: we
> understood that physical theory is neither a meta-
> physical explanation nor a set of general laws
> whose truth is established by experiment and in-
> duction; that it is an artificial construction, man-
> ufactured with the aid of mathematical

5. Pp. 178–179. See my discussion of Pascal and Kierkegaard, above, Chapter 2, pp. 74–76.

magnitudes; that the relation of these magnitudes to the abstract notions emergent from experiment is simply that relation which signs have to the things signified.

For the physicist the hypothesis that all natural phenomenon may be explained mechanically . . . has no meaning. *This proposition transcends physical method* (p. 280; Duhem's italics).[6]

Still we must recognize an innate contradiction in Duhem's philosophy — again something that was probably inseparable from the scientific language of his times. Here and there, on occasion, Duhem said that he was — an admittedly Catholic — "positivist." The meaning of "positivist" has been debated and may have changed since then; yet what Duhem meant was clearly stated in the admiring foreword by Louis de Broglie: "He believed instinctively, as all physicists do, the existence of a [physical] reality external to man." (As had Einstein).[7] In any

6. P. 277. Simone Weil (1942): When "the relation of the sign to the thing signified is being destroyed, the game of exchanges between signs is multiplied of itself and for itself. And the increasing complication demands that there should be signs for signs. . . . As collective thought cannot exist as thought, it passes into things (signs, machines . . .). Hence the paradox: It is the thing which thinks, and the man is reduced to the state of a thing." *Gravity and Grace,* New York, 1979, pp. 209–210.
7. Being a Frenchman, Duhem often referred to "logic" and to "laws." (I cannot recall who it was who said that "God did not intend to save His people by logic" — to which allow me to add my own prejudice [generated

case, Duhem believed and stated that physics was not only a symbolic and particular but a *separate* kind of knowledge from our knowledge of the world.[8] And the same Duhem who, on occasion, denied that he was a metaphysician ("No Metaphysical System Suffices in Constructing a Physical Theory" — one of his subchapter titles) ended his magisterial volume: "In a word"

> the physicist is compelled to recognize that *it would be unreasonable to work for the progress of physical theory if this theory were not the increasingly better defined and more precise reflection of a metaphysics; the belief in an order transcending physics is the sole justification of physical theory* (p. 335).

These are his italics.

Long before Duhem and Heisenberg there were of course numberless thinkers, poets, writers, skeptical of and rebelling against the optimistic pretensions of rationalists and scientists. They too believed in two separate realms of thought, the poetic

---

also because of my experience with unendurable Logic courses]: isn't logic hardly more than verbal mathematics or verbal geometry?)

8. Alas, this is also emphasized by Jaki in his *The Limits of Limitless Science,* Wilmington, 2000, p. 67: " . . . my resolve to save the sciences and the humanities from mutual encroachments, and, if I may add, leave whatever inspiration they may offer, in compartments that are at least methodologically separate." How odd that this priest, proponent of two *separate* kinds of knowledge, has the reputation of a bridge-builder between Science and Religion, recipient of the Templeton Prize of Science and Religion . . .

and the mechanical, or call it perhaps the romantic and the inorganic; they exalted (and often rightly and convincingly) the primacy, if not the priority, of the former. But few of them saw the connections; to them the two worlds were inimical *and* separate. Yet there were a few solitary exceptions who saw the connections with a stunning clarity. One of them was the Neapolitan Vico, who wrote, two centuries before Duhem: "The physical world is made up of imperfectly, infinitely divisible things." What science amounts to is a probabilistic kind of knowledge that has its own limits, due to the limitations of human nature; and its own limits are due to the mental axioms and operations of the scientists themselves. Their — by their nature mathematically and geometrically limited[9] — accuracy / certainty Vico called *certum*. But the *certum* is only part of the truth, of verity, of *verum*. "The distinction between the metaphysical and the physical is the same as that between the divine *verum* and the human *certum*." "*Certum est pars veri*." The second is dependent, indeed, *part* of the first.

And Tocqueville, in a private letter, 1858, a century before

---

9. "However free we might render our minds from the corruption of spirit and tongue, however perfect we become in the exercise of human reason, we can never hope to have complete knowledge of nature around us. God has made the world through his elements and his acts, so only He can know it in truth. The only things we can be said to make — fully make within ourselves, not simply reconstruct externally from God's creations — are the mathematical abstractions that do not involve physical body." Mark Lilla, *G. B. Vico: The Making of an Anti-Modern,* Cambridge, 1993, pp. 32, 76. Ibid., p. 13. Vico: "The young ought not be taught to attempt the application of geometry to life, an insane method."

Heisenberg's *Physics and Philosophy:* "A hypothesis which permits the prediction of certain effects that always reoccur under certain conditions does, *in its way* [my italics] amount to a demonstrable certainty. Even the Newtonian system has no more than such a foundation."

And now I arrive at the most dramatic proposition of this book. Contrary to all accepted ideas we must now, at the end of an Age, recognize that *we,* and *our earth,* are at the center of our universe.

We did not *create* the universe. But the universe is our *invention;* and, as are all human and mental inventions, time-bound, relative, and potentially fallible.

Because of this recognition of the human limitations of theories, indeed, of knowledge, this assertion of our *centrality* — in other words: of a new, rather than a renewed, anthropocentric and geocentric view of the universe — is neither arrogant nor stupid. To the contrary: it is anxious and modest. Arrogance and stupidity, or shortsightedness, are the conditions of those who state (and either believe or pretend to believe) that what frail human beings have figured out (most of these during the past five hundred years, a short period in the history of mankind!): that water *is* H_2O, that there *cannot be* speed greater than 186,282 mph, that $e = mc^2$, etc., etc., that these scientific and mathematical formulas are absolute and eternal truths, in every place and at any time of the universe, trillions of years ago as well as trillions of years in the future; that mathematics and geometry preceded the creation of the world (which is what Galileo and Newton implicitly, and on occasion explicitly, believed) — that these are eternally valid truths even before the universe existed and even if and when our world (or, indeed, the universe) will cease to exist.[10]

I ask my readers to hear my voice. A speaker cannot hear his own voice. He knows not only what he wants to say but *how* he wants to be heard (in this case, read), and *why;* but in this case, as well as in so many others, the *why* is implicit in the *how.* This book is not a scientific treatise, and not even a philosophical one. It is an essay (*OED:* "4. A short composition of any particular subject," "a finished treatise," "an undertaking"). It is an essay — an undertaking — of common sense. I appeal ("appeal": "call": "ring") to the common sense of my readers. It is an appeal to think — yes, at a certain stage of history — and I can only hope that for some people the peal may ring with at least a faint echo of truth.

When I, a frail and fallible man, say that every morning the sun comes up in the east and goes down in the west I am not lying. (I have been saying this to my students for many years, before I stumbled upon Duhem using the same example.)[11] I do not say that a Copernican or post-Copernican astronomer,

10. And that God himself was preceded by, and subordinated to, mathematics. Consider this astonishing statement by William F. Buckley Jr., the chief intellectual figure of American Catholic "conservatism": "Thomas Aquinas explained how it is that God cannot make two and two equal other than four" (in his op-ed piece in the *New York Times,* 21 January 2001, espousing and encouraging President George W. Bush). Thomas Aquinas said no such thing.

11. *Eppur si muove! Si. Il sole.*

stating the opposite, is lying. There is accuracy, determinable, provable accuracy, in his assertions: but, leaving aside the respective merits of different pursuits of truth, my commonsense experience involving the sun and the earth is both prior to and more basic than any astronomer's formula.

But there now exists an additional evidence of our central situation in the universe. Five hundred years ago the Copernican/Keplerian/Galilean/Cartesian/Newtonian discovery — and it *was* a real discovery, a real invention, a calculable and demonstrable and provable one — removed men and the earth from the center of the universe. And often with good intentions.[12] Thereafter, with the exponential growth of scientism, and especially with the construction of ever more powerful instruments, among them telescopes (instruments separating ourselves ever more from what we can see with our naked eyes — but of course the human eye is *never* really "naked"),[13] this movement led to our, and to our earth's having become hardly more (indeed, even less) than a speck of dust on the edge of an enormous dust-bin of the universe, with the solar system itself being nothing more than one tiniest whirl among innumerable galaxies. So many scientists — and not only scientists! — assert this, not at all humbly, but with a false intellectual pride. But the discovery, in the twentieth century, that the human observer cannot

12. Kepler: "The purpose of the world and of all creation is man. I believe that it is for this very reason that God chose the earth, designed as it is for bearing and nourishing the Creator's true image, for revolving among the planets."

13. Cassirer on Goethe vs. Newton: "The mathematical formula strives to make the phenomena calculable, that of Goethe to make them visible."

be separated from the things he observes (especially when it comes to his, unavoidably interfering, observation of the smallest components of matter) reverses this. We, and the earth on and in which we live, are back at the center of a universe, which is — unavoidably — an anthropocentric and geocentric one.[14]

But this is something both more (and less) than the returning movement of a pendulum. The pendulum of history (and our knowledge of the world) never swings back. It is due to our present historical and mental condition that we must recognize, and proceed from *not at all a proud but from a very chastened view of ourselves,* of our situation, and of our thinking — at the center of *our* universe. For *our* universe is not more or less than *our* universe. That has been so since Adam and Eve, including Ptolemy and Galileo and Descartes and Einstein and Heisenberg and my own dual, because human (opinionated as well as humble), self.[15]

Already more than four hundred years ago Montaigne wrote: "The question is whether, if Ptolemy was therein deceived, upon the foundations of his reason, it were not very foolish to treat now in what these later people [the Copernicans] say: and whether it is not more likely that this great body, which we call the world, is not quite another thing than that

14. Bernard D'Espagnat, *In Search of Reality,* New York, 1982, p. 21: "To some extent, Bohr undid what Copernicus had accomplished; he reinstated man at the center of his own description of the world, wherefrom Copernicus had expelled him."

15. Ortega y Gasset: "By origins, in development, and as an object, the entire material universe was 'historical,' so that natural science too (beyond history of science) can thus be historicized and 'humanized.'" Note that he goes beyond the history of science.

what we imagine."[16] And another fifty years later Pascal, who was a different thinker from Montaigne: "Thought constitutes the greatness of man" (*Pensées* 346). "Man is but a reed, the most feeble thing in nature; but he is a thinking reed. The entire universe need not arm itself to crush him. A vapor, a drop of water suffices to kill him. But, if the universe were to crush him, man would still be more noble than that which killed him, because he knows that he dies and the advantage which the universe has over him; the universe knows nothing of this. All our dignity consists, then, in thought. By it we must elevate ourselves, and not by space and time which we cannot fill" (347). "*A thinking reed*. It is not from space that I must seek my dignity, but from the government of my thought. I shall have no more if I possess worlds. By space the universe encompasses and swallows me up like an atom; by thought I comprehend the world" (348).

Yet for my purposes, and for the purposes of this essay, I must not rest content with these precious recognitions of the great seers of the past. My present argument about the centrality (and the uniqueness) of man in the universe must both rest on and proceed from their inseparability. And therefore I must shift my focus slightly from Copernicus, Kepler, Galileo, these astronomers at the beginning of the Modern Age, to the

16. Four hundred years later, *The Cambridge Encyclopaedia of Astronomy:* "Our calculations may be well done, but if our assumptions are wrong, our answers will be systematically in error. . . . Astronomers must make many assumptions and draw many analogies about objects far outside our normal experience. To appreciate the consequence of this necessary fact [I should say: condition] is to understand a frailty of every model of the universe."

philosopher Descartes: because in *some* ways, and on *some* levels the Copernican / Newtonian system remains workable, and, on a certain circumscribed level, still true — whereas Descartes's ideal of the scientific method, of the geometric mind, of Objectivity, of *cogito, ergo sum,* is not. (Pascal: "Descartes: useless and unreliable.") Three centuries later I tried to reformulate this: not *cogito, ergo sum* but *sum, ergo cogito* — or, rather, *sum, ergo cogito, ergo sum.* I exist; therefore I think; and the consciousness of my thinking gives yet another dimension to my existence.[17]

This — so obvious — priority of our existence to our thinking, and the inseparability of our thinking from matters around us, of what we can see and observe, is part and parcel of our central situation in the universe. This human inseparability of the knower from the known means the inevitable participation of the knower *in* the known (a participation which, unlike the admission of a participant into stocks or other riches, does not extend the quantity of what he possesses, while the very recognition of this limitation may extend the quality of his understanding).[18] Heisenberg put it simply: "There is no use discuss-

17. Simone Weil, *Gravity and Grace,* p. 54: "Although from a distance Descartes seemed to offer a coherent system befitting the founder of modern science, on looking into it more closely we no longer find anything but contradictions. . . . How could the man who had thus adopted the Socratic motto 'know thyself' devote his life to the kind of research into physics that Socrates scoffed at?"

18. Lilla, *Vico,* 48: Bacon "let his pride get the best of him, forgetting that it is our task to study physics in a speculative temper of mind, as philosophers, that is, curbing our 'presumption.' Unlike Bacon, Vico believes that we should study nature not to master it, but 'in order to curb our pride.'" Sir W. Waller in *Divine Meditations* (cited in Chesterfield's *Letters to His Son:* "Take me off from the curiosity of knowing only to

ing what could be done if we were other beings than we are." A half-century later the French physicist Bernard D'Espagnat remarked sadly that all the books and scientific treatises and even popularizations describing the indeterminism of quantum physics "have remained silent about this question of inseparability"[19] — or, to use my preferred word: participation. Thus D'Espagnat, a fine French physicist and thinker three and a half centuries after Descartes, at the end of the Modern Age: "Before constructing any kind of mental notion one must first — and at least — exist. Any kind of semantic argument about the word 'existing' cannot refute this elementary recognition. . . . Existing precedes knowledge [connaissance], one must exist in order to know [être pour connaître]."[20] *Sum, ergo cogito, ergo sum.*

Human knowledge is limited by the sensual and intellectual capacities of human beings. And yet, with all of these limitations, there exists still another condition, suggesting the human centrality. Human beings, including all of their frailty and fallibility, are the most complex organisms in the entire universe. This unique complexity is in itself an argument for our central situation. Among other conditions, this complexity includes the fantastic and often incredible — though, again, *not* limitless — functions of our imagination. It is our imaginative capacity

---

know, from the vanity of knowing only to be known, and from the folly of pretending to know more than I do know.")

19. D'Espagnat (with Etienne Klein), *Regards sur la matière: Des quanta et des choses,* Paris, 1993, pp. 172, 174: "It is astonishing that philosophers of science have, till now, given little or no attention to this inseparability." Which is, too (p. 77), "that quantum mechanics are *necessarily incomplete.*" P. 198: "we must concede that our physics are nothing but *human.*"

20. Ibid., p. 197.

which, together with memory, proves, among other things, that the laws of physics do not always and everywhere apply to the perceptions and functions of our minds. I attempted to illustrate such functions of memory earlier with examples of the complexity of the human mind; but there is more to that, since this complexity involves not only the functions of human memory but also the mysterious functions of human imagination. Human imagination anthromorphizes and humanizes everything, even inanimate things. We must recognize not only the powers but also the very limitations of our imagination: that our thinking of the world is unavoidably anthropomorphic, just as our exploration of the universe is inevitably geocentric. It is not only that "Know Thyself!" is the necessary fundament of all our understanding of other human beings. It is that we can never go entirely outside of ourselves, just as we cannot ever go outside the universe to look at it.

The sprouting of seeds in men's minds is miraculous in its causal complexities; the laws of physics do not always or necessarily apply. "The physical fact" wrote Paul Valéry, is that

> a drop of wine falling into water barely colors it,
> and tends to disappear after showing a pink
> cloud. But suppose now that some time after it
> has vanished, we should see, here and there in
> our glass — which seems once more to hold *pure*
> water — drops of wine forming, dark and *pure* —
> what a surprise! This phenomenon of Cana is not
> impossible in intellectual and social physics.

This, surely daring, anthropocentric assertion accords with what the American writer (and farmer) Wendell Berry writes about geocentricity, the marvelous — and miraculous — uniqueness of our earth, "our daily bread":

> Whoever really has considered the lilies of the
> field or the birds of the air and pondered the im-
> probability of their existence *in this warm world*
> *within the cold and empty stellar distances* will
> hardly balk at the turning of water into wine —
> which was, after all, a very small miracle. We for-
> get the greater and still continuing miracle by
> which water (with soil and sunlight) is turned
> into grapes.

The miracle, in this cold and frightening universe, is our warm earth; the miracle, in this world, is our human existence. (I could have written "uniqueness" instead of "miracle," because there is an element of miracle within anything in this world that is unique.)

Perhaps we should give a fleeting thought to the history of the word *world,* the history of ideas being inseparable from the history of words. In English and in other Germanic languages "world" comes from *wer* + *eld*, the "man-age" or "age of man."[21] (Which is one reason why the idea and the usage of the concept of "pre-historic" man may be nonsense.) Vico argued that hu-

---

21. In my native language "world," *világ*, is connected to "light."

man beings, having the capacity to understand, are citizens of the universe: *mundi civis sum,* he wrote (which is something quite different from *cogito ergo sum*).

In all of the foregoing I made few references to God. Three or four hundred years ago not only Copernicus and Kepler and Galileo but Descartes and Newton, too, had to make references to God, fulsomely and at times, I am inclined to think, honestly. (There is evidence that Isaac Newton did not believe in the Trinity. Did he know — did he recognize the obvious — that his system had reduced God to a constitutional monarch of the universe? Probably not: in any event, we do not know.) More than three hundred years later this little book is addressed to all kinds of readers. But the scarcity of my references to God was not a rhetorical device. What I wrote in the preceding few pages about our central situation in the universe can be understood and accepted by non-believers and by agnostics and atheists of many kinds.

But now, nearing the end, I can no longer exclude referring to God. And this is not easy. That God had something to do with creating *me* is not difficult to believe: a spark of such a cognition is potentially there within every human heart. But: "We do not understand the existence of the world one whit better by telling ourselves that God created it." And yet: "To believe in a living and personal God, in an eternal and universal consciousness that knows and loves us, is to believe that the

Universe exists for man."[22] And here our knowledge, our understanding, our very imagination stops. We cannot scientifically —
or logically — "prove" that God exists. But we cannot prove the
impossibility of God's existence either: because in the entire
universe the meaning of God may be the only meaning that
exists independent of our consciousness. Earlier in this book I
wrote about the limitations of the meaning of "fact." All I can
say here is that, for once, *factum* is both a precise and a final term
when and if it refers to *God* having *made* the universe — within
which the miracle of our existence is yet another example of
participation, and of our central situation.

According to Genesis (and also according to Plato) this
earth is the oldest of the planets. God created it *before* the other
planets and the "firmament." Of course this runs entirely contrary to what we know from science, from modern astronomy.
But the essence of this contradiction is, again, not physical but
metaphysical. I will not argue it further, except to state what is
fundamental (and obvious): Our earth is our home. There is a
special reason to insist on this at the time of this writing — not
only because of the, increasingly questionable, purpose of "ex-
plorations" of "space" and the, perhaps particularly American,
near-manic wish to believe in extraterrestrial beings and extraterrestrial intelligence.[23] There is a terrible restlessness all over

22. Miguel de Unamuno, *The Tragic Sense of Life,* London, 1923.
23. Seemingly believed and evidently talked about by a "Christian" and
"conservative" American president, Ronald Reagan, whose imagination
was attracted to the realm of *Star Wars.* I am referring not to his space
rockets program but to the evident effect of the movie *Star Wars.* In that

the world at this time, a mass migratory restlessness probably without precedent, destructive of many places and things, and perhaps of civilization itself (a word and an ideal that arose four hundred years ago, at the beginning of the Modern Age). About life on this earth Vico wrote, three hundred years ago, that the barbarian "learns to survive in nature but is incapable of making his home within it." A foundation of civilization is the appreciation of permanence of residence. The entire ideal of the *home,* and of *privacy,* was the creation not of the Middle but of the Modern Age. There may be a particular admonition in this for present-day Americans who divide, as Wallace Stegner put it, into "boomers, 'those who pillage and run,'" and stickers, "those who settle and love the life they have made and the place they have made in it."

That the pillagers are now called "developers," that the many millions who exchange their dwelling places as frequently as their automobiles (and spouses) are called "homeowners" is but another evidence of the present corruption of language. The corruption of language is both cause and effect of the current breakdown of communications. Consider the astounding duality of developments in our mass democratic age. On the same hand a near-fantastic extension of "communications" has come into existence — not only travel but the ability to talk to or

---

film there was no word of "God"; but there *was* a substitute for it, a "modern" religious term: "the Force." Men shooting out into space battles were "blessed" with the phrase: "May the Force be with you." This (like the "Evil Empire") appealed to Reagan. In one of his speeches he enunciated: "We are the Force. The Force is with us!"

read from or see or hear from people across the globe in a matter of seconds. On the other hand there exists the deeper, and more serious, breakdown of "communications" between people in everyday life: the deteriorating capacity, and willingness, to listen or to pay attention to each other.[24]

Throughout this little book I have insisted upon the importance of thinking — more exactly: on the present and increasing importance of thinking about thinking. But now I must go further than that — to say something not about thinking but about beliefs. This is not easy, because while thinking and believing are not the same, ideas and thoughts and beliefs overlap in our minds. And while — from evidence gathered from their various expressions — we may see and say something about what other people (and of course what we ourselves) think, it is more difficult, and in some cases perhaps even impossible, to ascertain not only the quality but the scope and extent of beliefs from various expressions of belief. Yet a brief description of this problem belongs within the concluding pages of this book,

24. Another duality, related to this increasing weakness of attention: on the one hand our communications (and our entertainments) have become more and more visual and less and less verbal; on the other hand the qualitative capacity of seeing has also deteriorated. The Gospel according to Matthew: "Thy eye is the light of thy body." Jacob Burckhardt: "Our eye is sun-like; otherwise it could not see the sun." Goethe: "We may imagine ourselves in any situation we like, but we always think of ourselves as *seeing*. I believe that the reason man dreams is because he should not stop seeing. Some day perhaps the inner light will shine forth from us, and then we shall need no other light." Note that color, too, is neither objective nor subjective but a synthesis of materials, of contrasts, and of the act of seeing.

since it is not separable from the earlier-mentioned complexity of human nature: a complexity that was ordained by God from the beginning, and therefore an existing condition (the condition that even honest non-believers may accept through a recognition that human nature does not essentially change). At the same time we must recognize that the complexity of thinking (including the constant increase of mental operations in large parts of a world where less and less work is physical) has been increasing—together with the increasing complexity of the structure of events, in plain English: with how things happen. Next to the recognition that "simple" people are now rare (though perhaps admirable) specimens in our days, we face the alarming condition that the minds of our children ("kids" in popular and repellent usage) have also become more and more complicated. This happens at the same time when puerility (demonstrating a gaping void of maturity) marks the expressions and the behavior of more and more people—including some of the recent Presidents of the United States. (The similarity of the phenomena of lingering puerility and of premature senility ought to be obvious.)

One consequence of this is the diminution of hypocrisy. Perhaps regrettably so: since hypocrisy was very pertinent to the now vanished Bourgeois Age. Hypocrisy may be the prevalent spiritual vice of a mature civilization. If it was "the tribute that vice pays to virtue" (La Rochefoucauld), it could flourish only in a society that understood the difference between vice and virtue, and felt compelled to pay tribute to the latter. More important: hypocrisy is evident in the difference between what people say and what they do, or between what they think and what they say. This means that they *know* what they *think*, but that it is their acts and not their intentions that matter (a condition less and less respected at the end of the twentieth century). (While the road to Hell is often paved with good intentions, the road to Heaven, too, is — or, rather, was — paved by many a bad intention that has not matured into an act.)

There exists now, at the end of the Modern Age, a difference not only between *what* people think but *how* they think; and a, perhaps yet deeper, difference between what people think they believe and what they really believe. This book cannot and does not and wishes not to include psycho-analysis, and especially not an analysis of religious beliefs. But for this writer who, in the end, cannot exclude a contemplation of God from his contemplation of our history, including our history of the universe, a few concluding statements are perhaps inevitable. One of them is that, yes, there is — probably — an evolution, not only of our churches and of our religion, but of our God-belief: an inevitable evolution not because the truth of God is relative but because our thinking, and our pursuit of Him, is fallible and historic. I sometimes think that this evolution, at least in the Western world, has gone through overlapping phases (always excluding many, many people, and not only saints). I wrote fifteen or so years ago:

> Why do I believe in God? Because such a belief comforts me? Or am I so skeptical of human beings that I do not want to have the universe ex-

plained by human reason alone? I believe because
I want to believe, and I know I ought to ask myself why I want to believe. This corresponds with
what I think about the evolution of the historian's
task. He ought not only to be concerned with
what people think. More important is the condition of *how* they came to think this or that —
within which the question of *why* they prefer to
think this or that is implicit. The evolution of
these questions corresponds with what I call the
increasing mental intrusion into the structure of
events — and possibly to the evolution of our religious consciousness. Roughly put, this evolution, to my mind, has gone through the following
stages: from the early, unselfconscious and often
animistic stage of the question: *What* is God? to
Who is God? to *Why* should I believe in God? (A
question of the eighteenth and nineteenth centuries in Europe, another version of which may
have been: What *can* I believe? — at which point
the Nietzschean recognition of the "death" of a
merely external God occurs) to the question:
Why do I want to believe? And this is inseparable
from another formulation of it: *How do I believe?*
the question honest believers must face in the
twentieth century. Within this question the inevitable, and largely salutary, increase of the recognition that religion is a matter of quality,

corresponds to a recognition that self-knowledge inevitably includes God-knowledge, at least to some extent. It also corresponds to the realization that we experience the world, *and* God, from the inside out as much as from the outside in.

What Nietzsche meant by the death of God was the fading of the presence of an external God. Yet Christ told us that God exists within each human being. God the Father is not a human being. We know that. Yet we must also be honest enough to admit that it is impossible to imagine God without certain human qualities knowable by us. This is due to the limitations of our minds and of our eyes, the other side of the coin being that it is also due to a divine element within us. I am no admirer of Calvin, but I found this quote from his Institutes: "Some sense of the Divinity is inscribed in every heart." In this sense Calvin, at the opening of the Modern Age, was a more modern and existentialist thinker than Nietzsche, who saw the passing of it.

Still, it is often easier to talk about God than to talk to God (and to listen to Him). Prayer requires attention, more than will. And we have sunk low enough so that in our world and in our times the dissolution of attention may cause even more troubles than the weakness of will.[25]

25. *Confessions of an Original Sinner,* New York, 1989, pp. 325–326.

In *The Tragic Sense of Life* Unamuno put it differently, and more clearly. "Faith in God is born of love for God — we believe that God exists by force of wishing that He may exist" — a dangerous statement; but then "and it is born also, perhaps, of God's love for us" (p. 150). Perhaps more telling and relevant to the main thesis of this book, is his implicit rejection of Cartesian logic: "The clearer our consciousness of the distinction between the objective and the subjective, the more obscure is the feeling of divinity in us" (p. 157). And this feeling of divinity is not, must not, cannot be the particular possession (and false pride) of believers. C. S. Lewis cites the words of the Scottish mystic George Macdonald (1824–1905): "There is no feeling in a human heart which exists in the heart alone — which is not, in some form or degree, in every heart."[26]

But C. S. Lewis also wrote:

> I think we must fully face the fact that when
> Christianity does not make a man very much bet-
> ter, it makes him very much worse. It is, paradox-
> ically, dangerous to draw nearer to God. Doesn't
> one find in one's own experience that every ad-
> vance (if one ever has advances) in the spiritual
> life opens to one the possibility of blacker sins as
> well as brighter virtues? Conversion may make
> of one who was, if no better, no worse than an
> animal, something like a devil. Satan was an

26. C. S. Lewis, *365 Readings,* New York, 1947, p. 53.

angel.[27] . . . We are denied many graces that we
ask for because they would be our ruin. If we
can't be trusted even with the perishable wealth
of this world, who will trust us with the real
wealth?

I think that this is particularly applicable to the dangers of a
spiritualist determinism whose shadows have begun to creep
over our world.

We have already entered a new age that will be (and already
is) quite different from the past — as well as from many of the
appearances still present. Christians may become — in many
countries they already are — a small minority. This is not something that can be ascertained by numbers, and not even by self-
identification or by habits such as church-going. These tell us
something but not much. One of the difficulties is ascertaining
the extent and the authenticity of belief (not only in others but
also in ourselves) is that even the acts and the words, not to

27. H. I. Marrou, *Saint Augustine and His Influence Through the Ages,* New
York, 1957, p. 76: "Satan is not an ANTITHEOS, a rival God: he is an
angel, fallen indeed, but an angel none the less who still retains his nature
and his impressive qualities." And at the same time: "The mightiest and
most perfect thing in creation, the thing nearest to God: the human soul in
its purest. For man *was* made in the image and likeness of God. . . . In the
human soul we *may* learn to discover the presence and the impress of
God" (the italics are mine).

speak of the unexpressed thoughts of people, often reflect their beliefs inadequately, if not confusingly. All of us have known many non-Christians who have acted in Christian ways, thus being *animae naturaliter cristianae*; and we also know many sincerely believing Christians whose expressions may show alarmingly non-Christian thoughts in their minds.

Whatever happens — not only to us but also to others — is inseparable from what we think happens. Often not for long; we may come to think about a past event differently. But what we think we believe is not always what we really believe. Our thinking — our ideas — will necessarily have their consequences. *Some* of our beliefs ought to.

A few pages before, and nearing the very conclusion of this small book, I made a perhaps startling but, I believe, not insubstantial argument for considering ourselves, and this earth, as the center of the — our — universe. (Our consciousness, which is always in time, cannot be separated from our consciousness of space.) And now — especially, but perhaps not exclusively for Christians — I must argue for the recognition of our central situation not only in *space* but also in *time*. In sum, that the coming of Christ to this earth may have been? no, that it *was*, the *central* event of the universe; that the greatest, the most consequential event in the entire universe has occurred here, on this earth. The Son of God has not visited this earth during a tour of stars or planets, making a Command Performance for us, arriving from some other place and — perhaps — going off to some other place.

And: only two thousand years ago! The arguments of Creationism against Evolutionism miss this essential matter. That matter is the unavoidable contradiction *not between "Evolution" and "Creation" but between evolution and history.* History: because in the entire universe men and women are the only historical beings; and because their own lives are not automatic, they are responsible because of their free will, of their choices.[28]

My argument does not only go against the obvious one: that the Survival of the Fittest is a doctrine thoroughly contrary to Christ's teaching of love. Darwinism is unhistorical, indeed anti-historical — even though its appearance was historical, coming at a time of unquestioned Progress. It elongated the presence of mankind to an ever-increasing extent, by now stretching the first appearance of "man" on this earth to more than one million years — yet another application of the optimistic idea of Progress? Those one million years before us — yes, before *our human selves* — imply that consequently there may be at least another million years still to come for us. Ought we not question this kind of unreflective shortsightedness — and not only because we have arrived at a time in history when men are capable not only of altering nature here and there but of destroying much of the world, including themselves? And, at least for Christians, does it not behoove them to rethink the essential meaning of their place

---

28. Allow me to repeat my earlier argument: we do not *have* ideas; we *choose* them. Consider the change of "public opinion" in Jerusalem from Palm Sunday to Friday. Which is why Christ did not condemn an entire people who, in the last moment, were reluctant to follow him. He knew very well how thinking involves choices: for what was the purpose of his parables? He taught people to think for themselves.

in history, concordant to the meaning of the appearance of Jesus Christ here on earth only two thousand years ago?[29]

Perhaps inexcusably, I have now gone beyond the scope of this book, the theme of which is the end of an era, and not the end of the world.[30] (Inexcusably, but perhaps unavoidably: because of the necessity, at the end of the Modern Age, to rethink the modern notion of "Progress.") This book is only a reminder of that.

29. According to the Darwinian scheme, a ridiculously asymmetrical point, a mere fraction of a second in the biological evolution of the world.
30. Pierre Duhem's authority in the study of thermodynamics was undisputed even by his otherwise ideological opponents. Yet he wrote about entropy: "By its very essence experimental science is incapable of predicting the end of the world as well as asserting its perpetual activity." *The Aim and Structure of Physical Theory,* Princeton, 1954, p. 280. To this let me add that the Christian view of the direction of history is necessarily teleological, leading to the First and then to the Second Coming. Nothing circular, nothing of (Nietzschean or Buddhist) Eternal Recurrence there.

Index